CONCILIUM

CONCILIUM 2004/3

THE STRUCTURAL
BETRAYAL OF TRUST

Edited by
Regina Ammicht-Quinn, Hille Haker and
Maureen Junker-Kenny

SCM Press · London

Contents

III. Consequences for Governance,
Canon Law and Pastoral Theology

Introduction

REGINA AMMICHT-QUINN, HILLE HAKER,
AND MAUREEN JUNKER-KENNY

The title of this volume, 'The Structural Betrayal of Trust' is meant to capture two dimensions of the sexual abuse crisis within the Catholic Church: the offences themselves which exploited the attitude of unquestioning trust and good will of children and parents towards their priests, and the subsequent experience of institutional denial, cover-up, hostility and juridical self-protection which they encountered when they had reached the stage, often many years later, of being able to report the crimes to the church authorities. On both levels we have to ask the painful question of whether there is a structural component, backdrop, or mentality that contributed to creating and handling the crisis?

The volume is opened by Marie Collins' account of her sexual abuse by a hospital chaplain and of her struggle with representatives of the institutional church to have her complaint heard and acted upon to protect still more children from being abused. The decision to 'break the silence' marks a new step out of the fate of having been made a victim.

The social psychological approaches in Part I offer perspectives from sociology, from brain and educational psychology, and from an analysis of race/ethnicity. The social theorist Nancy Nason-Clark investigates what is understood by sexual violence. Peter Adriaenssens treats the severe brain physiological and psychological effects of sexual abuse in general on children's development. Writing from the experience of his support centre for victims in a family setting, he outlines the motivation, goals and methods of this work of healing which aims at 'a new story of good parenthood'. The brainwashing children experience in their relation to their most significant others, their parents in their family home from which there is no escape, is a feature that appears with different elements also in the clerical abuse situation. The experience of being torn between the accusation of the perpetrators and self-accusation seems to indicate that within the structures of dependence that mark this age the way left for a child to react is to interiorize mistrust both towards these others and her own self. The sense of betrayal of a trust which a child can hardly afford not to offer is aggravated by feelings of shame and guilt. Further insight into the asymmetry of power relations between adults and children is offered in Traci West's analysis of the factors of race/ethnicity as additional power markers in stratified, more or less openly hierarchical societies.

Both the victim's account and the social theoretical analyses in Part I leave us with questions that reappear in the biblical, historical, theological and institutional reflections in Parts II and III.

– *Regarding sexual abuse as an exercise of power*: For the last two decades feminist studies on care have reflected the characteristics and the ethical value of asymmetric relationships against cultivating an abstract, individualist, 'duty-free' notion of autonomy. What anthropological, ethical, pedagogical and religious insights can help us to keep safe this process of mutual learning and growth between children and adults, between people in dependent situations and their powerful counterparts? In what ways is this vulnerable journey of anticipating in age-adequate ways the full exercise of their freedom susceptible to the danger of adults abusing their superior powers on children who are forced to submit to the terms of the relationship for the sake of their own physical and psychological survival and personal sense of belonging? What distinguishes sexual abuse from other such practices of domination? How does it play on children's fear of separation? How does the promise of closeness invade a growing child's sense of self as well as violate his or her existing values, world-view and outreach towards God? What confusion and despair does it add when the priest abuses his position as a trusted 'power broker' in relation to God?

– *Regarding the definition of victimhood*: Should the clear distinction between the sufferer and the offender be dropped and the latter included as a 'victim' in the wider sense, who suffers from the exploitation of sexual longing in a market-led culture and from an inadequate process of professional religious training towards celibate priesthood? How should the finding be evaluated that in contrast to sexual abuse in the family many of the abusing priests are not paedophile in the clinical sense of targeting children who have not reached puberty? Does the discrepancy between the skillful use of his adult and ordained authority to seek out children and youths at the beginning of puberty, and the light this throws on the stage of his emotional and sexual maturity justify the view that the moral perspective which imputes his acts as deliberate choices to him as agent is incomplete? Should the moral stance be extended to an invitation for reconciliation to a repenting offender both from a psychological and a Christian perspective? Aware of the trap that a self-serving psychological mechanism of scapegoating poses with its clear distinction of emotionally loaded figures of darkness from figures of light, what would be appropriate forms of insisting on the norm of a mature, responsible, non-manipulative expression of sexuality?

– *Regarding structures, categories and plausibilities specific to the Roman Catholic Church*: In view of their contribution to the mind-set, rationalizations, and practical opportunities of the abusers, what theological conclusions can be drawn for an access system to ministry based on obedience and chastity, on the exclusion of women and on an ontological difference to the lay people of God? Is there any extent in which passive service expectations of congregations and the lack of a sense of the need for scrutiny colluded in the one-sided distribution of power? How far are believers responsible for a church which in its authoritarian structures exploits unfulfilled longings – for transcendence, healing, union, victory over death? To what degree is every citizen implicated in a culture's excesses by tolerating market-enhancing addictions to sex, drink and dieting, and a fascination with violence extending to the creation of a new genre, religious horror films in the name of piety?

– *Regarding the future protection of children*: Is a 'zero tolerance' stance, as that now practised in the Roman Catholic Church in the United States, the best available measure that establishes beyond doubt the end of institutional protection for the perpetrators, or is continuing care and therapy a better way of protecting children in the future? Is the ambiguity of offering support to the offenders to be tolerated, or is a clean cut the only publicly acceptable form of institutional response? What kinds of co-operation between state law and canon law can be implemented?

Some criteria for coming to conclusions on these questions can be found in the biblical, historical, and theological reflections of Part II. Andreas Michel follows up the biblical sources that deal with sexual violence towards children and concludes that in the more than 200 texts in the First Testament in which violence against children is thematized sexual violence only plays a marginal role. To point out that a prohibition of child sexual abuse or incest is lacking in the Old Testament appears as anachronistic and as inadequate both for exegetical and ethical reasons. The text-hermeneutical problems begin, according to Michel, already with the concepts of 'childhood' and 'youth' which in the social history of the times of the First and Second Testaments cannot be separated out clearly. Michel discusses sexual violence against boys in connection with the lack of a prohibition of paederasty in the Ancient Near East; sexual violence against (pre-pubescent) girls is not mentioned, whereas violence against young women is treated in some texts in the context of the father's or husband's power of disposition over women. It is not possible to conclude from the lack of a prohibition of incest that it was allowed, as the religious condemnation of incest in Leviticus 18 indicates for Michel.

In his investigation of sexual violence as a violation of a specifically Christian demand to protect children, Hubertus Lutterbach points out that defending children from sexual offences was one of the great humanizing achievements of Christianity. Not only a fundamentally different understanding of sexuality in comparison with ancient Greece but above all the Christian esteem of children as the model of 'being a child of God' led to this marked change. The loss of credibility in the current crisis about the abuse of children in the church is all the more serious as its very own roots are betrayed. Eamonn Conway examines whether operative theologies of priesthood have contributed to child sexual abuse. After discussing evidence on the distinctive profile of clergy offenders, among a higher than average history of having themselves been abused as children, he contrasts two guiding concepts of understanding the priestly office: the *repraesentatio Christi* model underlines the distinction between priest and community, whereas *repraesentatio ecclesiae* captures the shared witness of the Christian community which is gathered and presided over by the priest. Linking the operative concepts with a recent empirical survey of the self-understanding of priests in several European countries, he is able to identify both risk indicators for abuse and the factors behind the predominant type of response from the hierarchy.

Part III on consequences for governance, canon law and pastoral theology is opened by John Beal's article on 'The crisis of ecclesial leadership' which became evident in the scandalous way in which sexual abuse was dealt with by church authorities. He also points to the *repraesentatio Christi* model of *communio*-ecclesiology, which neglects the significance of the Holy Spirit in a church committed to a Trinitarian structure. As a consequence, dissent and conflicts are too quickly transferred into terms of lack of loyalty and betrayal. In addition, according to Beal, it is the bureaucracy that mediates between Roman centralism and local churches that has to be blamed for the lack of communication. Its members serve both as a filter that keeps unwelcome information from the decision-makers, and as a channel through which information is passed to the respective local churches. This bureaucratic structure typical of hierarchical organizations does not promote alternative – consultative – structures of communication; it obstructs them, especially when uncomfortable truths have to be confronted, such as the sexual abuse of children and youths by priests. Instead of drawing the obvious conclusion that church and institution are not identical, the church is bent on 'purification' and the 'amputation' of those members that are diseased, even at the price that at times innocent office-holders are affected. Only by turning the existing structures of communication upside down so that the flow from below up to the top could be adequately installed, could the marginalization and demonization of critical voices within the church be ended.

The following two articles by Hans-Jürgen Guth and Rik Torfs deal with the specific measures canon law provides both at the levels of the universal and the local church. They agree that an adequate set of norms exists, the implementation of which, however, according to Rik Torfs, meets significant obstacles in the still pervasive concept of the church as *societas perfecta* and in a poor internal legal culture. For Guth, calling for stricter norms underestimates the scope of canon law that has existed in its codified form since 1917 and 1983, and since 1990 also for the Eastern churches united to Rome. In view of the procedures fixed in these codices Guth shows that the Catholic Church deals with sexual abuse of clergy and religious in the context of 'sins against chastity,' but without any explicit reference to the sixth commandment. The age limit of 16 years confirmed as late as 1983 shows how difficult it is for canon law to confront sexual violence against minors. The legal perspective is guided by the identity of the priest, without giving attention to the victim's perspective – the point is not to endanger the duty of sexual abstention. Guth traces the transfer of legal responsibility for sexual abuse to the Congregation for the Doctrine of the Faith in the '*motu proprio*' of 2001, in contrast to the usual regulation for crimes in which diocesan bishops are responsible for clergy while the pope is responsible 'only' for bishops and cardinals. He critiques that local bishops, besides contributing to the culture of secrecy and cover-up, are often not familiar with the procedural possibilities of canon law which can refer to state courts and which raised statutory limitations to ten years as recently as 2001. In his critical comparison of different German with the North American regulations Guth insists that only through openness and transparency in the implementation of existing legal norms can trust be regained.

The thesis that the churches of the West have to learn to live in the ruins of their power systems is put forward by Rainer Bucher in his reflections on 'Body of Power and Body Power. The Situation of the Church and God's Defeat.' One feature of this state of affairs is that priests, although privileged within the church in many ways, have to live in a post-modern society with a largely pre-modern theory of their priesthood. Pastoral care as the creative confrontation of the present and the Gospel destroys itself in situations of abuse. The lost social power of church and priesthood is reclaimed at the most intimate of places. The God who is proclaimed in this way is not a God of salvation and of solidarity with the powerless but an idol of power. Thus sexual abuse within the church is part of 'God's defeat within God's church'.

In their concluding comments, the three editors reflect on a personal basis as female lay theologians and mothers insights and demands for future church policy and theological reflection.

Breaking the Silence: The Victims

MARIE L. COLLINS

I was twelve when I was admitted to a children's hospital with osteomyalitis. I was a happy child, successful and popular at school, outgoing and confident. I never had any reason to distrust an adult and knew nothing of sex. I was totally unprepared to cope with the abusive events to come and the confusion of feelings they brought with them.

Fr Paul – the Catholic chaplain, a young man a couple of years out of the seminary – visited me soon after my admission. Religious sisters ran the hospital and the adults around me treated Fr Paul with the deepest respect. He was very popular with the children but visited me more than the others. I felt privileged that such an important man wanted to be my friend. I was in pain, nervous and lonely, but Fr Paul seemed to understand how I was feeling. He spent time listening to me talk about how I missed my family and my fears about my operation. He made me feel I was his special friend. I trusted him completely. Now I realize that he was gaining my confidence – 'grooming' me for what was to come.

When he began to touch me intimately I was shocked and confused. I felt instinctively that what was happening was wrong. I tried to stop him but my protestations were met with arguments I could not counter. He told me if I thought the 'game', as he had introduced it, was wrong I 'was not normal'. He 'was a priest, and priests could not do wrong'! It may seem strange now but to a child of that time this rang true. He said I was 'confused'. If I was thinking anything was wrong, then I had 'right and wrong mixed up'. When I continued to protest he would resort to saying I was 'stupid'. He made me feel I was the one in the wrong and I was being unreasonable. His arguments repeated over and over convinced me: I was stupid and somehow what was happening was my fault.

In my last week Fr Paul stood at the end of my bed with his camera and intimidated me into allowing him to take an intimate photograph, a photograph taken for one purpose only – the sexual gratification of the viewer. As he took the picture I felt degraded and humiliated. The following morning was the day of the weekly confessions. Fr Paul stood at the end of my bed again, a prayer book in his hands in place of the camera, his stole around his shoulders – pious and authoritative – how could he not realize the hypocrisy of it? I wanted so much to confess how 'bad' I had been, but I knew he would be annoyed so said nothing. This left me feeling worse. A conscientious Catholic, I had made my confirmation only a few months before; I had now made a 'bad confession'.

My abuser had power and authority – he was an adult, I was a child. It was an unequal struggle. He exploited my vulnerability, my dependency, and my innocence. My parents and the hospital had entrusted me to him in the expectation that my welfare would be his priority; but to Fr Paul, his perverted needs justified his betrayal of their trust. He used his priesthood to facilitate his abusive behaviour.

I left the hospital after three weeks a very changed child. Guilty and confused, I *knew* I was a bad person and I didn't want anyone to find out. I went back to school no longer confident or happy. I was constantly anxious and withdrew into myself. I was a bad person, but if I didn't let people get close, they wouldn't know. I was convinced it had all been my fault, something bad about me had made it happen. I became depressed and would not go out to play. I just wanted the world to go away.

My closing in on myself affected my interaction with others, and family relationships suffered greatly. I turned away from my brother to such an extent that we became estranged for many years. At 17, I went out with a boyfriend for the first time. It was during this friendship that I was first hospitalized with psychiatric problems. I suffered acute symptoms of anxiety and was prescribed tranquillisers. This was the beginning of a lifetime of medication and hospitalizations needed to keep me functioning.

I held down a job for a number of years, controlling panic attacks and depression with medication. Marriage to a good and supportive husband and the arrival of a fine son brought some normality for me. Unfortunately it didn't last. At 30 I had to give up my career when I began to suffer from agoraphobia. Years followed where others had to do the simplest things for me – take my son to school, shop for groceries – while I remained a prisoner of my fears. My feelings of worthlessness were always there. I felt I was an inadequate mother and wife. During bouts of severe depression I would be hospitalized. Often at these times I felt my family would be better off without me. I saw myself as nothing but a nuisance. Later, during therapy it became clear all these problems arose from the abuse.

Twenty–five years after the abuse, I spoke of it for the first time while undergoing psychoanalysis. My doctor worked hard to help me accept that it was not my fault. Eventually I felt strong enough, even though it was the hardest thing I had ever had to do, to report to the church what had happened. I wanted them to know in case my abuser was still in a place of trust with children. I went to a senior curate in my parish. The curate responded by telling me I had probably been to blame for my abuser's actions and refused to take his name or report him. This devastated me completely and threw me back into my well of guilt. I could not bring myself to speak of it again. Over the next ten silent years, I suffered further hospitalizations with depression. Apart from the effect the curate's rejection had on me it left children at risk.

The Irish media highlighted paedophilia in 1995 and I felt I must try again to report my abuse. I wrote to the Archbishop of Dublin and to the hospital where I had been a patient. The hospital immediately offered any help I needed, including counselling. The church sent me a letter suggesting I contact a solicitor and asking that I telephone for an appointment to make a report. This response foreshadowed the legalistic attitude that was to prevail over all else in the way the church dealt with my case and is still dealing with cases. I just wanted to make the church aware that one of their members might be a danger to children. Thoughts of solicitors or claims had not occurred to me, but the church's first reaction was to direct me, not to therapeutic care but to a solicitor!

At this time I was a practising Catholic and had high expectations of how the church would deal with my report. I expected them to care about what had happened to me and to act quickly to ensure no children were left in danger. As time went on I began to realize there was little concern for me. I was considered a nuisance, a threat, and eventually the enemy!

When I met the Chancellor of the diocese to make my report, I was told that Fr Paul's file had been checked and no complaint had ever been made about him before. I felt this, along with other things said, was intended to deter me from making a report but I proceeded. I was then left for five months with no contact. These five months were an extremely difficult and distressing time. When I spoke again to the Chancellor, I was told that Fr Paul, within days of my report, had admitted the abuse, but the Chancellor had been too busy to get back to me! I was also told his file had been re-checked, and it was found he had been guilty of abuse in the past. I was told Fr Paul had been immediately removed from his parish and the church had reported my case to the police. I asked if the Gardaí had been told of his admission and his past record. I was assured they had.

Later, when I spoke to the police I discovered that none of what the church official had said about contact with them was true. The church had not reported my case. The hospital had made a report, but when approached by the Gardaí, the Chancellor had refused to make any statement about Fr Paul except to confirm he had been chaplain in the hospital. When the Gardaí discovered from me that he had admitted the abuse and had a history of offending on his church file, I had to make a new statement. I gave them a letter I had received from the Chancellor confirming Fr Paul's admission of guilt. When the Chancellor heard this he was extremely angry with me and threatened to sue me for handing his letter to the police. I was upset at this threat and not knowing what my legal position was, I employed a barrister. He told me that what I had done was perfectly correct and I should continue to co-operate with the civil authorities, giving them any information I had. Next I learned that Fr Paul had been left in his parish – where one of his duties was preparing the confirmation class – for months after I reported him before he went on temporary leave. His appointment to the parish was only withdrawn a year later when he was arrested. It would appear the church, despite knowing his guilt, were hoping it would all blow over and he could go back to work without his colleagues or his parishioners knowing the danger he posed to children.

By now I was disillusioned and very hurt. I was already going through a lot of emotional turmoil as any victim does on reporting their abuse after such a long time. Instead of having my church support me in this difficult time, they were protecting my abuser. I was being lied to and threatened by them because I was co-operating with the Gardaí. A curate in my parish, who was helping me, was moved away and told by his superiors not to talk to me because he was beginning to question how my case was being handled.

This cold, defensive position of the church was maintained as the Gardaí case was developed against Fr Paul. I requested and was granted a meeting with the Archbishop. I asked him if it was morally right to refuse to co-operate with the Gardaí when he knew I had been abused, when he knew Fr Paul had admitted to being an abuser. The Archbishop's response was that, despite Fr Paul's admission, he was entitled to his good name and could not be considered guilty until found so in a court of law. This meant that if the case didn't get to court, he could be returned to ministry and contact with children. The Archbishop maintained he had to follow his legal advice – if this conflicted with what was morally right it did not seem to matter. I pointed out that the Irish church's own guidelines on the issue were being ignored (*Child Sexual Abuse: Framework for a Church Response*, p. 15, see also 4.6.6). These state 'the fundamental presumption of innocence must be upheld and respected, *unless the contrary has been established*. Fr Paul's admission of guilt had established the 'contrary' in my case. The Archbishop responded that these were only 'guidelines' and as such were not binding.

This was despite the fact that the laity in the diocese had been assured they were being followed to the letter.

A second victim was uncovered during the Gardaí investigations. This second case lent weight to mine and Fr Paul was charged with both. After a legal process, he was found guilty on all counts and served a jail sentence. The day he was convicted, the Archbishop issued a statement to the press saying the diocese had been 'co-operating' with the Gardaí. I challenged the honesty of this statement and was told by the diocese that it was justified because they had not said they had been 'co-operating *fully*'. The laity were being deliberately misled by this cynical manipulation of facts.

This became a turning point for me; I decided I could no longer trust my church, no longer have any respect for an institution which had been part of my life for over forty years. Shortly afterwards I learned concerns about Fr Paul's interaction with children in his parish had been reported to the diocese only the year before my report. The curate to whom I reported initially was not disciplined for failing to take action – in fact he was promoted. Soon after the trial he was appointed parish priest in the very parish in which Fr Paul had been a curate for twelve years prior to his arrest. Without any retraining in how to handle victims since he had shattered me years before, he was now in a position where more recent victims of the same abuser might be approaching him with their disclosures. Did the church show any care for them?

When a television documentary was being planned about my story, the church authorities refused to take part. They threatened legal action if it was broadcast, as they contended it was untrue, that I was lying. Despite this effort to silence the media, my story did become public. Sustained media pressure and anger among the laity brought me an apology from the Archbishop and an admission that my criticisms were justified and the decision not to co-operate with the Gardaí had been a mistake (Dublin diocese 13.4.02). This statement was worded very carefully. An example of this is a sentence saying Fr Paul had not been removed from his '*house*' for four months after my report. A reader would be led to believe by this that he was not in his parish, but living safely in his house away from children. In fact he was working as normal in his parish for those four months, so why use the word 'house' instead of 'parish'? Yet another instance of self-protection by minimizing – and in the process misleading the laity once more as to the truth of a situation.

I went through a couple of years of therapy after the court case, which helped me to reclaim my life, to regain a feeling of self worth and self-confidence. Slowly I came to terms with what had happened to me and to my life. In the years since then my depression has not reappeared. I don't look back with bitterness on how different my life might have been had Fr Paul not crossed my path – there is no point. I have forgiven him; he was a man with a problem. The actions of my church are harder to forgive. They took their decisions in the cold light of day. They decided their priority: the protection of the institution. Showing God's love to one who was hurt and protecting the vulnerable appeared nowhere on their agenda. This has been shown to be the norm in many similar cases by the recent Irish church report *Time to Listen – Confronting Child Sexual Abuse by Catholic Clergy in Ireland.*

I am still struggling to regain the trust and respect I once had for the Catholic Church. I am sad that I have not yet returned to being a fully prac- tising Catholic. My religion was not taken from me by my abuser but by the church itself. I am not alone in this. Alienation from the church has hap- pened to victims and family members 'because of the way their complaint of abuse was responded to and managed rather than as a direct result of the abuse *per se*' (*Time to Listen – Confronting Child Sexual Abuse by Catholic Clergy in Ireland*, p. 201).

The church must admit the mistakes of the past to learn from them. The time has come for a complete re-evaluation of the structures and ethos of the institution. In this closed all-male society, should there be a place for women? Can an all-male group understand and reflect the needs and feelings of a society which is 50% female? In marriage, male and female complement each other to make the whole. The church opposes divorce, as both partners are so important to the well-being of the family. Yet in the church we have a male clergy divorced completely from any female dimension. Surely this disables them in their decision-making for their 'family' – the faithful. We have seen abusing priests moved from parish to parish by their superiors hoping to keep the scandal quiet while ignoring the young lives in their hands. Would women have left children at risk so easily? I doubt it. Critics sometimes say that women are influenced by their feelings too much. Unfortunately it is a grave lack of feeling for victims and vulnerable children which has led to the church's present crisis.

The precept that protection of the institution is paramount has to be challenged by those within the church. This focus on the avoidance of 'scandal' at all costs has led, in the case of clerical child sex abuse, to enormous damage to the institution that the hierarchy sought to protect. The mishandling has caused more people to walk away from their religion than any 'scandal' would ever have done.

It appears to the ordinary faithful that there is only one morality that matters to the church and that is sexual morality. The church seems to be obsessed with it. Child abuse has little to do with sex; it is a crime of power and violence. The majority of abuse happens in the family home behind closed doors, yet we hear sermons on the evils of homosexuality, contraception etc. and none on the evils of spousal violence or child abuse. How much are children valued by the church? Quite rightly no effort is spared to prevent abortion but when a child does come into this world is that child valued enough?

There has to be better communication at all levels. The church needs to take a deep look at itself and see that it is losing its ability to communicate with the people. The days of issuing edicts and receiving unquestioning compliance have gone, even in Ireland. Times have changed and rather than refuse to accept this, efforts have to be made to discover how to change with them. The church must move into the twenty-first century and realize that trust and respect now have to be earned and can no longer be taken for granted.

The laity have to be heard, their questions answered, their views heeded. Priests also have to find a voice. I have met many priests who are afraid to speak up, afraid to disagree with the actions of their superiors, to seek change because of fear that their future career might be affected negatively. How can a church be healthy if those within it fear to speak? Anyone who truly has the welfare of the Catholic Church at heart must have courage and work for change. Open the doors and let in the light!

I. Social Psychological Approaches

What is Sexual Violence?

NANCY NASON-CLARK AND LANETTE RUFF

Again I saw all the oppressions that are practised under the sun. And behold the tears of the oppressed, and they had no one to comfort them. On the side of the oppressors there was power, and there was no one to comfort them (Ecclesiastes 4.1).

And whosoever shall offend one of these little ones that believe in me, it is better for him that a millstone were hanged around his neck, and he were cast into the sea (Mark 9.42).

There are many ways to speak of sexual violence. It includes violence of a sexual nature that occurs within the confines of a relationship with an intimate partner. It includes date rape, or sexual assault by a stranger. It includes attempted or forced sexual intercourse that occurs as a result of armed conflict, or mass rape.[1] It includes the demand of sex for survival:[2] in the global trafficking of human persons, as in the sex slave trade, or treating women as 'territory' to be conquered or plundered, as in times of war. It can occur in refugee camps, in prisons[3] or amongst domestic or migrant workers. It knows no geographical boundaries. Its pain and devastating impact cross all borders.[4] Often sexual violence involves children and in these instances it is commonly referred to as child sexual abuse.

> About 234,000 convicted sex offenders are under the care, custody, or control of corrections agencies on an average day. Nearly 60% are under conditional supervision in the community (US Department of Justice, February, 1997, NCJ-163392).

> According to the National Child Abuse and Neglect Data System, an estimated 9.6% of confirmed or substantiated child abuse and neglect cases in 2001 involved sexual abuse. This figure translates into nearly 1.2

child sexual abuse victims for every 1000 children under the age of 18 <www.americanhumane.org, accessed 08/03/2004>.

A study conducted for the National Institute of Justice found that 13 % of female adolescents and 3.4 % of male adolescents have been sexually assaulted (US Department of Justice, April, 1997, The Prevalence and Consequences of Child Victimization).

Persons age 12 and older experienced an average annual 140,990 completed rapes, 109,230 attempted rapes and 152,680 completed and attempted sexual assaults between 1992 and 2000, according to the National Crime Victimization Survey . . . Female victims accounted for 94% of all completed rapes, 91% of all attempted rapes, and 89% of all completed and attempted sexual assaults, 1992–2000 (US Department of Justice, August, 2002, NCJ 194530).

Finding No. 3: *The investigation did produce evidence that widespread sexual abuse of children was due to an institutional acceptance of abuse and a massive and pervasive failure of leadership* (Office of the Attorney General, Commonwealth of Massachusetts, July 23, 2003, 'The Sexual Abuse of Children in the Roman Catholic Archdiocese of Boston,' Executive Summary, p. 3).

Writing about family violence, Miedema and Nason-Clark (2004) claim that it is a complex and multi-faceted issue, involving violations that are, for the most part, gendered. It is not merely personal, but also a consequence of social inequality and in that sense it is, in part, socially constructed. It impacts victims at a deep and enduring level, with consequences to their social well-being and emotional and physical health, enduring long after the abuse has stopped. As a result, its impact is far-reaching, extending into many private and public spheres of life. It must not be taken lightly: it has the power and potential to change the life course of individuals and families.

Disclosures, charges and convictions of child sexual abuse in the United States, Canada and elsewhere have radically altered congregational life too – the power and prestige of the office of priest has been shattered and the public image of the contemporary Roman Catholic Church tarnished. Few – priest and parishioner alike – have been left untouched by the recent media attention given to what some errant clergy have done to children behind the closed doors of the church, orphanage or youth centre (cf. Jenkins 1996). As a result, the secondary victims are impossible to count. Some have left the church forever. Some have left and returned, but without their children

(Nason-Clark 1998). Some have stayed and worked through their grief in private. Others have called out publicly for the church to respond in compassion to victims and their families. All would agree that there is no turning back of the clock. What once was hidden is now in public view. The proverbial church carpet has been rolled up, exposing the dirt underneath. As a result, sexual violence perpetrated by men who have taken vows of poverty and obedience, not to mention celibacy, has created a public outcry, amongst those inside and beyond the walls of the church. In terms of outrage, there is no separation of believers and non-believers.

Citing statistics from around the world, Kroeger and Nason-Clark (2001) argue that when sexual violence is perpetrated by a father, uncle, brother, grandfather or another adult relative, the victim must sort out myriad feelings, ambiguities and contradictions. They write: the victim 'may feel both love and hate'. Often the victim is economically dependent on the abuser or fears reprisal should a disclosure be made.

At other times the violation occurs not at the will of a family member but by a trusted adult – a coach, teacher, or religious leader.

Betrayal is still a central feature of the abuse, the sense of trust that has been broken and it is almost impossible to exaggerate the vulnerability the victim feels. The trusted relationship, then, provides both an opportunity for the abuser to exploit and also increases the likelihood that the victim will keep the abuse a secret.

In *Erotic Innocence: The Culture of Child Molesting* (1998), James Kincaid argues that few stories in our culture are as news-generating as those of child molesting. Sensational cases involving actors, like Woody Allen, and pop stars, like Michael Jackson, receive much press and publicity. So do stories of teachers and scout leaders. In one chapter of his book, 'Perversion among the Prominent', Kincaid claims that clerics molesting children is the best occupational story that journalists have in their tool kit. Some of the most graphic examples of sexual abuse, highlighted by the media, take place in a boarding school environment, or in other residences where children are involuntarily placed, like youth training centres or orphanages. From the Canadian film *The Boys of St Vincent* to television documentaries from CNN, the sentiment is the same: how could a priest, a holy man, called of God, molest innocent children.[5] Some have described the sexual violence of clergy as a 'cancer' (Benyei 1998), others as a 'crime' (Shupe 1998). Whether we rely on a medical model or the criminal justice system, the fact of the matter is clear: religious institutions are in crisis as a result of what some have described as the most pressing issue facing organized religion in the contemporary world (Jenkins 1998).

I. Defining child sexual abuse

The way child sexual abuse is defined is not just an academic exercise. It is extremely important for a number of reasons, not least of which include the ability to bring offenders to justice. For attempts to assess the true level of child sexual abuse is dependent upon such definitions, as are public and institutional policies to stop it and to respond compassionately to its victims.

First, and foremost in any definition, is the notion that the victim is a child and the perpetrator is an adult. Then there is the issue of consent. Most jurisdictions consider that there is a legal age for consent, though they may differ at what age they believe consent for sex actually occurs. Based upon these two points alone, then, one can assert that child sexual abuse is non-consensual sexual activity that occurs between an adult and a minor. Finkelhor (1984) rightly refutes the notion that sexual activity between children and adults *can* be freely entered into and fully consensual; for sex to be consensual, a person must know what they are consenting to and have the freedom to say either yes or no. Finkelhor presents convincing evidence that children are not in a position to give free consent to an adult asking for sexual gratification and the short and longer term consequences of such sexual activity reveals both its devastating nature in the life of the child and its concomitant impact on their adult sexual lives. Thus, definitions of child sexual abuse must refer to the age of consent of a child, include both intra-familial and extra-familial abuse, refer to any activity that is for the sexual gratification of the adult, and also be inclusive of non-contact activities such as exposure to obscene or pornographic material (Colton and Vanstone 1996).

According to Benyei (1998: 62–3), child sexual abuse encompasses any sexual contact with a minor including fondling; undressing; exposure, or peeping; vaginal or rectal penetration, fellatio, or cunnilingus; inappropriate sexual hugs and kisses; or suggestive comments. She argues that a useful guideline for considering grey areas, like hugging, is whether or not the minor feels uncomfortable with the behaviour and/or threatened by it. Child sexual abuse can happen in the family setting, where the victimizer may be a parent or step-parent, a sibling, a cousin, a grandparent or an uncle. Or, it can occur amongst non-family members, where commonly the person is involved in some form of care taking or trusted role with the child, such as a coach, a boy scout leader or a priest/minister (Kinnear 1995).

In cases of child sexual abuse, victims are forced or coerced into compliance with the sexual wishes of the perpetrator sometimes by the manipulative offers of gifts or inducements, but mostly through the victimizer's power of position, which also presses them into secrecy. There are other factors that impact upon whether or not a victim will disclose their abuse, including their loyalty to the person who has abused them (and their fear of a loss of relationship once the disclosure has been made); the perception of guilt, that they are personally responsible for what happened; a fear that they will not be believed and that they will suffer humiliation and perhaps other consequences as well for having told their story of violation; and personal denial, since the painful events are simply too emotionally difficult to face in full view (cf. Benyei 1998; Finkelhor 1984; Bross, Krugman, Lenherr, Rosenberg and Schmitt 1988). For some victims, skeletons in the closet seem preferable to the possibility of public or private humiliation as their story is dismissed or they are accused of lying; Benyei (1998) refers to this process as scapegoating.

Finkelhor (1984) argues that four conditions must be met for sexual abuse to occur: factors relating to the offender's motivation to abuse a child sexually; factors relating to an offender overcoming the internal inhibitions to sexual abuse; factors leading an offender to overcoming external inhibitions; and factors leading the abuser to believe the child will offer little resistance. The interplay between internal and external factors indicates the multi-disciplinary nature of any sustained solution to this major social problem.

As a field of study, sexual offending – including both offenders and victims, as well as measures to combat its frequency and severity – has been a growing area of inquiry. The subject matter has interdisciplinary appeal, which means that a variety of 'different constituencies are competing with each other to claim and explain the phenomenon of the sex offender' and to proscribe appropriate intervention for both offender and victim (Thomas 2000:15). Explanations vary from the press, the public and elected politicians, to those whom society regards as 'experts' in matters of sex or abuse: therapists, physicians, scholars and activists. Explanations vary from a simplistic view of the offender as a 'monster' to notions about childhood victims learning to become adult offenders. To be sure, one discipline alone cannot be responsible for understanding all the dynamics giving rise to child sexual abuse, nor can one group of professionals alone be responsible for solving it. It will take sacred and secular resources, working in concert with one another, to end the sexual violation of children, whether the victimizer is a parent or a priest.

It is important to note that the impact of child sexual abuse often extends well beyond the victim to others in their family or friendship networks.[6] When abuse occurs within the confines of a faith community, the secondary victims include other parishioners, church staff and (perhaps) seminarians as well (cf. Nason-Clark 1998; Benyei 1998; Kroeger and Nason-Clark 2001).

II. Is sexual violence a recent phenomenon?

It is not uncommon to hear people ask whether sexual violence is a rather recent phenomenon, a product of modernity as it were. The answer to this question is no: what is new is that disclosures are no longer immediately dismissed, nor are perpetrators' actions simply hidden from public view. Jenkins (1998) claims that child sexual abuse by clergy in the Roman Catholic Church have 'caused unparalleled damage to the prestige and credibility' of the church, its leadership and the rank-and-file priests.[7] At least until the late 1980s, Catholic authorities adopted an approach that was both secretive about the abuse and apparently unsympathetic and failing in compassion towards victims and their families (Jenkins 1998). Offences were simply dismissed (and then erased from organizational memory) and the offending priests were moved to what was believed to be a less tempting context in which to represent God to the people and the people to God. As Jenkins so correctly states: 'this optimistic approach was unfounded and a few priests survived to become serial molesters of epic proportions' (p. 118).

To be candid, clergy sexual malfeasance is not a recent invention (Shupe 1998). Rather, sociologist Anson Shupe claims that even historians of mediaeval Europe[8] have observed the fertility of the religious ground as it related to the potential of sexual violation within the inequitable power relations demonstrated within the Roman Catholic Church. Tracing the history of child sexual abuse beyond the confines of the Christian church reveals that 'forcible rape' has been common throughout history (Brownmiller 1975), as have some attempts at prosecuting the perpetrator of such offences (Myers, Diedrich, Lee, Fincher and Stern 2002).

But, especially brutal has been the abuse of religious power. Using the term clergy malfeasance, Shupe (1998) claims that in 'crusades, witch hunts, inquisitions, and pogroms, history shows us a dark side' to religious power. Sometimes that manifests itself as 'the exploitation and abuse of a religious group's believers by trusted élites and leaders of that religion. In legal terms such malfeasance represents a violation of fiduciary responsibility' (p. 1). Ultimately those who trust their leaders most, who place them on a pedestal, are more vulnerable to exploitation and abuse – sexual and otherwise – than others.

Across the globe, child molestation is one of the most hated crimes in the criminal system (Briggs 1995: xiii). In her book, *From Victim to Offender: How Child Sexual Abuse Victims Become Offenders,* she argues that many victims become perpetrators, repeating the behaviour that they hated when they were in the victim role. Based upon data collected amongst both incarcerated and non-incarcerated men, Briggs reveals that all but one of her study participants who were convicted of child molestation claimed that during their childhood they had suffered prolonged periods of sexual violence at the hands of at least one adult and that prior to this study, they had not defined their experiences as sexual abuse. History repeats itself: the cycle is perpetuated. That is one of many reasons why it is so important for not only the safety of individuals but also the protection of our wider society that the response to child sexual abuse is swift. Perpetrators need to be called to justice and accountability as certainly as victims and their families need therapeutic intervention. Otherwise, the pattern of abuse will in all likelihood continue.

While sexual abuse is not recent, there are some ways in which our modern technology has created some new forms of violation. In her 2001 article, 'Child Predators on the Web', Debbie Mahoney claims that 'child predators are forming an online community network and virtual bond that is unparalleled in history. The paedophile now has the ability to disguise identity, thus enabling believable presentation as a member of a teen group. This disguise enables the paedophile to target potential victims. Intrusions into the private world of the child and teenager also provides a quick means of tracking down information on potential victims with very little effort . . .' (p. 81). Given the ever-changing technological advances in our culture, new means for violating children can be just a mouse click away.

Religious and secular components of our culture must be on their guard to ensure that child victims are protected and that adult victimizers are brought to justice. One of the first steps on the healing journey of any victim of violence is disclosing the personal circumstances of violation (Nason-Clark and Kroeger, forthcoming). According to Rod Tobin (1999) in *Alone and Forgotten: The Sexually Abused Man,* there are three major reasons why sexually abused males avoid disclosures of their past violations: (1) the negative judgment by family members and loss of friendship; (2) stigma in the eyes of society; and (3) lack of understanding by therapists and unpleasant experiences in therapeutic settings (p. 12). In *How Long Does it Hurt? A Guide to Recovering From Incest and Sexual Abuse for Teenagers, Their Friends, and Their Families,* Mather and Debye (1994) point to the need to highlight for teenagers that the abuser is always responsible for the abuse. Since one of – if not *the* – biggest question a child or teen asks in the aftermath of sexual violence is 'Why?' it is important never to excuse the abuser or take away the perpetrator's personal responsibility for the acts committed. Supporting victims as they journey towards healing and wholeness is not only the mission of the Christian church, but ought to be the responsibility of every believer. Churches ought to be not only sacred spaces, but safe places as well.

III. Concluding comments

Sexual violence always implies a power differential between the abused and the abuser, the victim and the perpetrator. This is compounded in cases involving an adult and a minor – what is commonly labelled, child sexual abuse.

No Christian believer – lay or ordained – has been left unaffected by the power and impact of the sexual abuse by religious leaders recently high-lighted by the media. Some would argue that the attempts to cover-up the abuse have created a far greater scandal than the sexual violations of priests, no matter how detestable and completely inexcusable these acts may have been (Nason-Clark 1998). In the long-run secret keeping is more damaging than the original incident that gave rise to the perceived need to maintain silence (Benyei 1998). All believers – but especially those vested with desig-nated offices of church leadership – have a role in stopping any attempts to encourage a 'holy hush' as it relates to the interface between religion and violence.

Notes

1. See V. Nikolic-Ristanovic, 'Living Without Democracy and Peace: Violence against Women in the Former Yugoslavia', *Violence Against Women*, 1999, 5, pp. 66–80.
2. See S. Brittle, *Youth Involvement in Prostitution: A Literature Review and Annotated Bibliography* (No. rr2001 – 13e), Ottawa: Department of Justice, April 2002.
3. See Amnesty International, *Breaking the Chain: The Human Rights of Women Prisoners* (1999). Retrieved March 8 2004 from www.amnesty.org/ailib/int-cam/women/report4/html.
4. Despite the devastation of sexual abuse, the National Child Abuse and Neglect Data system estimates that 61% of rapes and sexual assaults are not reported to police.< www.americanhumane.org, accessed 08/03/2004.>
5. See *The Boys of St Vincent*, Canadian Broadcasting Corporation 1993; written by J. N. Smith and produced by National Film Board of Canada.
6. See B. J. Carter, *Who's to Blame? Child Sexual Abuse and Non-Offending Mothers*, Toronto: University of Toronto Press 1999.

7. Investigative staff of the *Boston Globe*, *Betrayal: The Crisis in the Catholic Church*, Boston: Little, Brown and Company 2003.
8. Anson Shupe cites Emmanuel Le Roy Ladurie as one example (1998: 5).

References

American Humane (2003), *Fact Sheet: Child Sexual Abuse*. Retrieved 3 March 2004 from www.americanhumane.org/site/PageServer?pagename=nr_fact sheets childsexualabuse

Benyei, C. R. (1998), *Understanding Clergy Misconduct in Religious Systems: Scapegoating, Family Secrets, and the Abuse of Power*, New York: The Haworth Pastoral Press.

Briggs, F. (1995), *From Victim to Offender: How Child Sexual Abuse Victims Become Offenders*, St Leonards, NSW: Allen and Unwin Pty Ltd.

Bross, D., Krugman, M., Lenherr, D., Rosenberg, D. and Schmitt, B. (1988), *The New Child Protection Handbook*, New York: Garland.

Brownmiller, S. (1975), *Against Our Will: Men, Women and Rape*, New York: Simon and Schuster.

Bureau of Justice Statistics (Greenfeld, LA) (1997), *Sex Offenses and Offenders: An Analysis of Data on Rape and Sexual Assault*, Washington: US Department of Justice.

Bureau of Justice Statistics (Rennison, C. M.) (2002), *Rape and Sexual Assault: Reporting to Police and Medical Attention, 1992 – 2000* (No. NCJ 194530), Washington: US Department of Justice.

Colton, M. and Vanstone, M. (1996), *Betrayal of Trust: Sexual Abuse by Men Who Work with Children*, London: Free Association Books.

finkelhor, D. (1984), *Child Sexual Abuse: New Theory and Research*, New York: Free Press.

Investigative staff of the *Boston Globe* (2003), *Betrayal: The Crisis in the Catholic Church*, Boston: Little, Brown and Company.

Jenkins, P. (1996), *Pedophiles and Priests: Anatomy of a Contemporary Crisis*, New York: Oxford University Press.

Jenkins, P. (1998), 'Creating a Culture of Clergy Deviance' in A. Shupe (ed), *Wolves Within the Fold: Religious Leadership and Abuses of Power*, New Brunswick, NJ: Rutgers University Press, pp. 118–32.

Kincaid, J. R. (1998), *Erotic Innocence: The Culture of Child Molesting*, Durham: Duke University Press.

Kinnear, K. L. (1995), *Childhood Sexual Abuse: A Reference Handbook*, Santa Barbara: ABC-CLIO.

Kroeger, C. C. and Nason-Clark, N. (2001), *No Place for Abuse: Biblical and Practical Resources to Counteract Domestic Violence*, Downers Grove, IL: InterVarsity Press.

Mahoney, D. (2001), 'Child Predators on the Web' in C. A. Anraldo (ed), *Child Abuse on the Internet: Ending the Silence*, New York: UNESCO Publishing and Berghahn Books, pp. 81–83

Mather, C. L. and Debye, K. E. (1994), *How Long Does it Hurt? A Guide to Recovering from Incest and Sexual Abuse for Teenagers, Their Friends, and Their Families*, San Francisco: Jossey-Bass Publishers.

Miedema, B. and Nason-Clark, N. (2004), Introduction in M. L. Stirling, C. A. Cameron, N. Nason-Clark & B. Miedema (eds), *Understanding Abuse: Partnering for Change*, Toronto: University of Toronto Press, pp. 1–19.

Myers, J. E. B., Diedrich, S. E., Lee, D., Fincher, K. and Stern, R. M. (2002), 'Prosecution of Child Sexual Abuse in the United States' in J. R. Conte (ed), *Critical Issues in Child Sexual Abuse*, Thousand Oaks: Sage Publications, pp. 27–69.

Nason-Clark, N. (1998), 'The Impact of Abuses of Clergy Trust of Female Congregants' Faith and Practice' in A. Shupe (ed), *Wolves Within the Fold: Religious Leadership and Abuses of Power*, New Brunswick, NJ: Rutgers University Press, pp. 85–100.

Nason-Clark, N. and Kroeger, C. C. (forthcoming), *On the Road to Healing: A Resource for Abused Christian Women*, Downers Grove, IL: InterVarsity Press.

National Institute of Justice (1997), *The Prevalence and Consequences of Child Victimization* (Research in Progress Seminar Series), Washington: US Department of Justice.

Office of the Attorney General, Commonwealth of Massachusetts (2003), *The Sexual Abuse of Children in the Roman Catholic Archdiocese of Boston: Executive Summary and Scope of Investigation*, Boston: Office of the Attorney General, Commonwealth of Massachusetts.

Shupe, A. (1998), 'The Dynamics of Clergy Malfeasance' in A. Shupe (ed), *Wolves Within the Fold: Religious Leadership and Abuses of Power*, New Brunswick, NJ: Rutgers University Press, pp. 1–11.

Thomas, T. (2000), *Sex Crime: Sex Offending and Society*, Cullompton: Willan Publishing.

Tobin, R. (1999), *Alone and Forgotten: The Sexually Abused Man*, Carp, ON: Creative Bond Inc.

Child Abuse: How Normal
Development is Disturbed

PETER ADRIAENSSENS

Children are dependent on those who bring them up. In a positive sense, this means that they acquire knowledge, emotions and social values in a safe milieu. But it also means that all kinds of things can go wrong between parents and child. Child abuse often occurs. Figures vary, depending on the definition of physical violence, neglect and sexual abuse used. On average at least one child in ten is a victim.[1] Probably this is a serious underestimation. A good deal of research shows that large groups of children fail to be recognized as the victims of child abuse because they do not meet the 'criteria' of excessively legal definitions. Researchers note that doctors, teachers, therapists and other helpers leave 50% of victims of physical child abuse and 75% of those suffering from emotional neglect undisturbed and unreported because they are 'slightly to moderately serious cases'. In the case of sexual abuse things are no better. At most 10% of the real number of young victims are identified. For the majority of them, around 80%, the perpetrator is someone known to them, usually a member of the family.[2]

I. Child abuse causes damage

Physical violence against children usually starts before the age of six, while sexual abuse starts above all between the ages of seven and twelve. That this results in damage which affects development is not surprising and marks a fundamental difference from violence experienced by adults after a safe youth.

There is now increasingly better documentation of how child abuse leaves traces in the brain and interferes with the development of a child at a moment when very important foundations are being laid. If we think of the development of the child as a house under construction, this means that during the laying of the foundations a hurricane occurs which breaks or damages some pillars of the house. Despite this natural disaster the construction goes on, but without repairs being made. The house becomes one whose shortcomings the inhabitant will feel all his or her life: damp walls, cracks in the structure because the house is moving, bad insulation, and so on. And when repairs are carried out, big mistakes made during the building will be discovered time and again. The foundations have not been laid as they should have been. A developing child is such a house in scaffolding. And even the damaged child or his or her helper cannot stop the growth; there is no pause during which it is possible to make thorough repairs. I shall briefly sketch out three levels where we now have evidence of a link between child abuse and brain damage.[3]

1. Child abuse damages the network of nerve cells and thus the intelligence

In the last ten years it has become increasingly clear how child abuse has an impact on the development of the brain. It is not surprising that babies are particularly vulnerable here. The size of the brain increases more during the first year of life than at any other time in life. During the first years of life there is a spectacular growth of the nerve cells which together form networks. For this to happen the young child must experience healthy stimulation. If it does not, for example if the parent is a drug addict, or there is a family situation in which there is a good deal of violence between the partners, or the child is sexually abused, the growth stops; nerve cells may even break away. The consequences are serious: an adult who is regularly aggressive towards a young child attacks the intelligence of the child, and robs it of the opportunity to learn to control its emotions and behaviour well. Such a lack can then translate later in life into compulsive behaviour, heightened obstinacy, hyper-activity, aggression or other psychiatric disturbances to be found in children. The perpetrators will often seize on these symptoms as an excuse for their behaviour.

2. Child abuse attacks the memory

Damage to the structure of the brain is increased by an abnormal production of the stress hormone. Child abuse is a source of great fear and stress. And that sometimes calls forth an appropriate physiological answer, which is coupled with a heightened production of the stress hormone (cortisone). Brains are not designed to grow in a bath of this hormone. It leads to the loss of cells in certain brain structures, which attacks the quality of the memory. Researches here provide the first evidence that the changing explanations of victims and the mistakes which are found in their story rest on the consequences of damage through child abuse; they cannot therefore simply be explained as the result of manipulation, induction or lying.

3. Child abuse damages the emotional intelligence

Child abuse also affects a third level in the brain, which is the core of the control of emotions, the amygdala. These see to the release of 'flight/fight hormones' which can bring the whole body into action. The amygdala form a kind of crisis centre which with difficulty controls all incoming stimuli. When that alarm goes off, it results in an emotional storm.

The amygdala are fully formed at birth. They continue to be strongly influenced by impressive, shocking and chronic experiences. Child abuse is the clearest illustration of this. In the period during which it takes place the amygdala are activated to an extreme degree. Consequently the victim lives biologically and psychologically in a constant state of the 'flight/fight' pattern. The hyperactivity of the amygdala continues, even though the danger has passed. Their effect cannot be regulated, as a result of which later in life the victim wrongly finds many circumstances frightening or dangerous.

4. Signs of child abuse are symptoms of mistakes in construction

So the impact of child abuse goes further than the damage which in due course may possibly become visible. The quality of life can be attacked long after the insecure situation is brought to an end. The many emotional and behavioural difficulties that we see with abused children, which are summed up under the term 'post-traumatic stress disorder', are not purely a psychological or emotional reaction. They are the expressions in behaviour and emotion of the mistakes of construction in the brain which are the result of child abuse. This motivates us to tackle risk factors at an early stage or to stop existing child abuse at an initial phase, since even an early stage of child abuse has a pernicious influence on the development of the brain. This is better than waiting for the clearly visible effects of abuse (the 'tangible evidence'), which are really symptoms of damage already done that is far more difficult to remedy.

II. The perpetrator brainwashes the child and attacks the foundation of any healthy relationship: a sense of solidarity and trust

Those who abuse children usually choose a child who already has a degree of vulnerability. Often the following elements are found in the victims:

– children of parents who have many conflicts with each other;
– children of parents who are addicted to alcohol or drugs, who abuse medication or have serious emotional disturbances;

- children who are socially isolated or turned in on themselves;
- the presence of a stepfather;
- a mother who is often absent from home a great deal and does not supervise family life;
- children who have bad contacts with their parents;
- parents who leave the care of their child a great deal to others and do not pay much attention to it;
- children who are hyperactive or have a difficult temperament;
- children with a mental handicap.

Moreover the way in which the perpetrator goes to work affects above all the psychological development of a growing child. Every child must find a way to integrate the two images of the parent ('the 'good' mother who cherishes and the 'bad' mother who is cross) into two partial aspects of the same person. The perpetrator claims to be acting 'for the welfare of the child' yet does things which are felt by the child to be shameful and humiliating. This split in the perpetrator hinders integration in the child. The child lives in constant fear of losing the kindness of the perpetrator-parent yet at the same time experiences fear of what it feels to be bad. Here the perpetrator damages the foundation of the relationship between adult and child: trust in those bringing up the child, adults, and belief in itself. The child evolves towards a split personality. On the one hand it is a good child who experiences positive relations with others and has a good image of itself; on the other hand it also has the opposite features: the bad self-image of a negative child who experiences frightening, frustrating and aggressive relations with others. This results in the child usually thinking in black and white terms: either it feels good and thinks nothing of the rest of the world, or – and this happens far more often – it feels bad and sees all the others as exceptionally good. As a result of a split the pendulum constantly swings between good and evil.

Those who do violence to a child interfere not only with the body but also with the spirit and the development of their victim. Brainwashing goes with violence. Perpetrators give their actions a pedagogical character by presenting them to the child as normal or as in the child's interest. Those who succeed do this 'so that the child does better at its lessons and behaves better'. Sexual abuse is presented as initiation. Physical and sexual violence are always coupled with emotional violence: the motivation of the violator for his actions must make it clear to the child that there is no reason for the adult to explain, and if there is a problem it lies with the child. This heightens a child's sense of being bad. This process reinforces the bonds of loyalty between the child and the perpetrator. Judith Herman calls this a traumatic bond.[4] Perpetrator and victim form a traumatic two-in-one.

We can conclude that children and young people who are the victims of child abuse experience three kinds of consequences: they often have a prior vulnerability, and they show signs of attacks on their brain structure and on their psychological development.

III. Who are the perpetrators?

Most perpetrators have a family life; they are employed or participate in voluntary work and are members of respected organizations. Some are admired by parents for the way in which they deal with children. When a carer is accused of sexual violence, there is often a counter-action by people who are convinced that there must have been a mistake, since they 'know this person very well and it is quite impossible that he could have done such things.'

The age of the perpetrators varies widely. Adult perpetrators are on average around thirty, but one-third of all perpetrators are minors. Most adult perpetrators show their first deviant behaviour before the age of eighteen. The number of adolescent perpetrators being treated for sexual abuse against children is increasingly markedly. There are striking similarities between minors and those who are of age.

Most of those who commit child abuse, at least 80% of them, are males. They are primarily fathers, followed by stepfathers. Brothers and cousins form a rapidly growing group which inflicts physical, emotional and sexual violence. Only a minority of all males who commit sexual abuse do so with children. Finkelhor and Lewis reckoned that between 4% and 17% of the male population have at one time abused a child.[5] Little is known of female perpetrators as a group. Their behaviour is usually simply called 'mothering' or 'a case of excessive maternal love'.[6] However, female perpetrators often collaborate with male perpetrators, work as baby-sitters, or seek systematic relations with adolescents. Female perpetrators have a preference for younger children than male perpetrators prefer, and they turn more towards children whom they know than towards unknown children. But the seriousness of the facts shows no difference from male perpetrators.[7]

IV. The consequences

Numerous investigations show that abuse in youth can lead to a broad spectrum of emotional, behavioural and relational problems. These can have consequences which appear quickly or long-term effects.

1. Consequences in childhood

The most frequent complaint is post-traumatic stress disorder. This embraces problems like nightmares, anxiety, feelings of isolation and the impossibility of enjoying ordinary everyday activities, with psychosomatic complaints, a fixed gaze and guilt feelings. Among children this can also be expressed in difficulties in concentrating at school, and in unusual reactions of terror which are prompted by incidents which recall their traumatic experience. In the main, children with post-traumatic stress disorder go into denial. But however well they may be able to suppress their thoughts at a conscious level, bodily reactions usually escape their control: sweating, twitching of the muscles, palpitations, a desire for pain and self-wounding. These are most probably connected with hormonal and other biological processes in the brain and in the body.

In addition there is a spectrum of psychopathology. Gomes–Schwartz found a clinically significant pathology among 17% of four- to six-year-old victims, 40% of seven- to thirteen-year-olds, and 8% of fourteen- to eighteen-year-olds.[8] Others found internalized disturbances (like depression and self-isolation) in 36% and externalized problems (like anti-social behavioural disturbances) in 38%. Moreover Finkelhor concluded that around 40% of maltreated and abused children seen by clinics would have pathological disturbances.[9]

2. Long-term consequences

Consequences can last into adulthood. Anxiety and depression are the most important complaints among adults who have been victims as children. Moreover a whole series of further psychiatric disorders can be present. Most studies conclude that around 30% of adults who were sexually abused as children show serious psychopathology in adulthood. Research has demonstrated that it is above all situations in which maltreatment of children goes on from an early age and lasts a long time which give the greatest risk of serious long-term disturbances.

V. The Confidence Centre: a vision of the provision of help in child abuse

In Flanders we looked for an answer to child abuse in which the welfare of the victim was put first. There is no obligation to report the abuse. But society expects current norms to be respected, while care is given to every person in need. If that can be done by providing help, that is good; if necessary an appeal must be made to the law.

In the 1980s, as a response to this challenge we developed the model of a Confidence Centre.[10] The public is invited to make contact ('in confidence') if any child abuse occurs in the family circle, or if someone knows of a victim of child abuse. The family in which the violence occurs is of central importance. Child abuse usually takes place within a particular relationship of nurturing. If one takes no account of these underlying patterns of behaviour, one risks simply shifting the problem elsewhere (another child outside the family becomes a victim, there is a move to psychological violence in place of physical violence, and so on). That does not mean that the violence is glossed over by 'understanding what is going on'. The Confidence Centre has a normative function: a child cannot be abused. The unjust situation for the child and the abuse is identified. Once this course has been taken, a second course can also be indicated. What has happened to a parent or parents that has led to such behaviour? The difficulty is above all not to follow a one-sided course, whether by regarding the parent(s) as criminals or by striking everything out of the parents' past. In the tradition of giving help, the Confidence Centre thus responds to a suggestion of child abuse with an offer of help. But this is not value-free. We look at the situation from the perspective of the child and help the abusing parents to move away from their own perception and recognize the suffering of the other party (the child). We put the relationship between parent and child in a confrontational framework. Actions arise out of the conviction that there are sound values in the perpetrator which can be spoken to and which can once again be put into practice. Through a confrontation in which the action of the parent is clearly called 'child abuse' we create space for a positive development. The prohibition of abuse results in a paradox: the parent must use his freedom of choice to achieve the loving relationship with the child which he desires. We strive for the best possible outcome, and here the first condition is the restoration of security for the child.

When the Centre was established in 1986, 3% of the children were reported to us by members of the family (the rest by professionals); in 2002 this was almost 50% (of the 1000 children a year who have been reported to the Centre). The story of which we constantly remind society (through publications, the media and lectures) persuades more and more people to follow this example.

For us, providing help begins with a recognition of the facts by the perpetrator(s). Victims have less chance of suffering long-term consequences if they get this recognition. Just as we assign an important place to confrontation in our methods, so too the recognition of responsibility for actions, the recognition of guilt, is a priority, in order to correct the traumatic two-in-oneness of the child and the perpetrator. Those who recognize that they have abused their child feel an existential fear of being damned. Most abusers are themselves children with unhappy experiences of youth. They are afraid to speak the truth because as children they learned that the answer was punishment and humiliation. The chance of a corrective experience lies in the relationship with the helper. The helper listens to the story of the abusing parent and with the parent seeks how a new story can be constructed, a story of good parenthood. Those who confront and express their guilt prove to the helper to be parents who remain honest. A bond arises in the relationship between perpetrator and helper, which stimulates the growth of a development that has got stuck. The attitude of the helper also makes it clear that we do not restrict the facts to mere physical or sexual violence but look at the broad basis from which a perpetrator abuses power in order to dominate, humiliate and damage a child. This life was a vicious circle; collaboration results in a spiral movement.

Of course not everyone can achieve this movement. In a quarter of situations the perpetrator will not recognize the situation, and we have to be true to our values. This means that we ourselves report the situation to the authorities. Providing help does not bring 'forgiveness' unless it achieves good, unless the child is recognized as a victim and is able to find security.

Translated by John Bowden

Notes

1. N. Draijer, *Seksuele traumatisering in de jeugd. Gevolgen op lange termijn van seksueel misbruik van meisjes door verwanten*, Amsterdam 1990.
2. D. Finkelhor, 'Epidemiological Factors in the Clinical Identification of Child Sexual Abuse', *Child Abuse & Neglect* 17, 1993, pp. 67–70.
3. D. Glaser, 'Child Abuse and Neglect and the Brain: A Review', *Journal of Child Psychology and Psychiatry* 41, pp. 97–116; F. W. Putnam, 'Ten-Year Research Update Review: Child Sexual Abuse', *Journal of the American Academy of Child Adolescent Psychiatry* 42.3, March 2003, pp. 269–78.
4. J. Herman. *Trauma en herstel*, Amsterdam 1990.
5. D. Finkelhor, I. A. Lewis, G. Hotaling and C. Smith, 'Sexual Abuse in a National Survey of Adult Men and Women: Prevalence, Characteristics, and Risk Factors', *Child Abuse & Neglect*, 14, 1990, pp.19–28.
6. J. Saradjian, *Women who Sexually Abuse Children: From Research to Clinical Practice*, Chichester 1996.

7. M. M. Rudin, C. Zalewski and J. Bodmer-Turner, 'Characteristics of Child Sexual Abuse Victims according to Perpetrator Gender', *Child Abuse & Neglect,* 19, 1995, pp. 963–73.

8. B. Gomes-Schwartz, J. M. Horowitz and A. P. Cardarelli, *Child Sexual Abuse: The Initial Effects,* Newbury Park, CA 1990.

9. D. Finkelhor, 'Is Child Abuse Overreported? The Data Rebut Arguments for Less Intervention', *Public Welfare* 48, 1990, pp. 23–9.

10. P. Adriaenssens, L. Smeyers, C. Ivens, and B.Vanbeckevoort, *In vertrouwen genomen,* Tielt 1998.

The Factor of Race/Ethnicity in Clergy Sexual Abuse of Children

TRACI C. WEST

When clergy sexual abuse occurs there is a violation of the psyche. Victim-survivors of the abuse have their spiritual and emotional identity raided by the perpetrator. The clergy perpetrator may use intimidation, shame, isolation, terror, trust, or scripture, among many other means. These emotional and spiritual dynamics of clergy sexual abuse are not only interpersonal (between the two people involved); they also include social dimensions that help to perpetuate the destructive impact of the abuse in fundamental ways.

Dynamics related to gender, race/ethnicity, sexuality, and class infuse the interpersonal interactions involved as well as the long-term effects of clergy sexual abuse for the victim-survivor. These interrelated social dynamics are part of the manipulations of the clergy perpetrator and the responses of the victim-survivor, but exactly how and to what degree each plays a role varies according to the specific situation of the abuse. In addition, the social meanings attached to gender, race/ethnicity, sexuality, and class centrally inform the religious institutional context of the sexual abuse and how its significance is interpreted. In the aftermath of clergy sexual abuse the trauma for the victim-survivor is often reinforced by the community's response to it (e.g. by their own family members, church leaders, criminal justice system). Therefore, his or her experience of intimidation, shame, isolation, terror, trust or the use of scripture in clergy sexual abuse is always shaped by a combination of emotional, spiritual, as well as social dynamics.

Highlighting understandings of gender and race/ethnicity in US society, I want to focus on this intertwined psychosocial impact. My inquiries concerning race/ethnicity and racism refer mainly to African American examples, and my discussion of gender concentrates on the traumatic experience of abuse perpetrated by males. How do these psychosocial dynamics in clergy sexual abuse of children and women constitute moral harm? When the interests and needs of victim-survivors are our primary concern, what factors must be included to address the perpetuation of this moral harm in our society?

I. Recognizing psychosocial dynamics

Unfortunately there is a general tendency to separate the psychological impact of intimate abuse from the social. In his study of sexual misconduct by Catholic priests, psychiatrist Len Sperry asserts that sexual misconduct can be conceptualized as: 'a psychiatric disorder, a crime, or an immoral act'.[1] For Sperry, treating clergy sexual abuse as a psychiatric disorder maintains a personal focus while treating it as a crime and an immoral act indicate a communal focus. He rightly believes that personal and communal impacts should both be attended to. However, usefully to conceptualize and address clergy sexual misconduct I believe it is necessary to go beyond this step. An approach that assumes a basic distinction between the personal and communal impact is insufficient and misleading. Our conceptualization of moral wrong has to be altered fully to include the destructive consequences of abuse labelled as personal (the psychological and spiritual dimensions). And those 'personal' consequences must be understood as completely intertwined with communal dynamics. Our most basic conceptualization of the problem of clergy sexual abuse also has to be shifted so that we move beyond a solely individualistic focus on the psychiatric disorder, crime, or immoral act of the clergy abuser to recognize institutional and societal collusion with the abuser, which indicates a broader, systemic problem of moral harm.

Recognizing how the victim-survivor's anguish involves a personal dimension that cannot be separated off from social (and institutional) concerns provides a starting point. Acceding to a false dichotomy dividing the personal from the social (and institutional) masks crucial dynamics of the abuse. When, for instance, we pay attention to issues of gender, we refuse to ignore that maleness is one of most consistent characteristics of clergy perpetrators across groups of Catholic and Protestant perpetrators and common in the experiences of both male and female victim-survivors. Thus we might ask what kind of institutional power does maleness have in the church that may intensify or reinforce the intimidation, for example, of the person being abused? What social meanings of maleness connected to the particular clergy abuser contribute to the anguish of the person victimized by the abuse? The kind of power assigned to maleness in the church (vested in God and male clergy) affects: how the abuser gains spiritual and emotional access to the victim-survivor; how the victim-survivor feels able/entitled to respond to the abuser; and the impact of the abuse in terms of how it is interpreted by the person abused, the church, and the wider community context.

Exploring the significance of gender within the impact of clergy sexual abuse is so key, in part, because of the centrality of gender in the church's system of authority and understanding of power. This is obvious in the Roman Catholic and Orthodox insistence on the theological necessity for an exclusively male clergy. It is apparent in the emphasis on acknowledging God as Father, which is primary in Christianity's trinitarian understanding of God and maintained across all traditions of the church. For example, to curb the slight but growing use of inclusive language for God used in liturgical settings, my own nine million-member denomination, United Methodists, reinforced rules during the 1990s about language in official liturgies of the church. They wanted to ensure that the trinitarian language used in baptism and ordination services referred to God exclusively as 'Father'. To ask about the meanings of maleness that may be part of the anguish of victim-survivors of clergy sexual abuse is to explore institutional (and social) culpability. It means inquiring about how the church's deeply entrenched understanding of moral authority is implicated in the abuse.

In addition, issues of race/ethnicity must not be ignored. In particular, they are vital to any discussion of clergy sexual abuse by Catholic priests in the United States. As psychologist Nanette de Fuentes writes:

> The more than 61 million members of the Catholic Church in the United States create a rich mosaic of diverse racial, ethnic, and socio-economic backgrounds . . . For example, the Los Angeles Archdiocese, one of the largest in the nation reports serving Mass in some thirty-seven languages . . . It is not uncommon for a parish that is primarily Latino or African-American to have priests in residence that are Irish, filipino, or Vietnamese. However the issue and importance of diversity, ethnicity, and race in the literature on victim-survivors of clergy sexual misconduct has almost entirely been overlooked . . .[2]

A much more thorough investigation of the implications of this racial/-ethnic diversity is needed than I will attempt here. But when consideration of the role of issues of race and ethnicity is neglected, our understanding and ability to address the problem of clergy sexual abuse is diminished.

Furthermore, in US society racial dynamics saturate issues of power, especially institutional power. More investigation is needed of how, for example, the white maleness of a perpetrator is part of the intimidation he wields against the victim-survivor. Or, how might the response of his church members to complaints made against him be informed by the Latino maleness of a perpetrator and the intimidating, inescapable presence of societal assumption about white superiority? The complex ways in which maleness is raced helps to provide important information about the impact of abuse on those directly effected by it as well as how its significance may be interpreted.

In news reports about sexual abuse of children by Catholic clergy there have already been some discussions of gender related to issues such as: why more men than women have come forward with complaints of abuse that occurred when they were children and youth; whether boys are more available targets of abuse for priests than girls; or if boys are more often chosen by serial perpetrators than girls because more clergy perpetrators may be male homosexuals.[3] This coverage consists mainly of a search for gender patterns and trends. Focussing on the role of gender in intensifying the victim-survivor's anguish instead forces us to investigate more precisely what is morally wrong about clergy abuse. It leads us to confront the question of how gender *should* function institutionally (and socially) so that it is not a supporting ingredient in the perpetuation of abuse.

When revealed by the authors of clergy sexual abuse accounts, how can racial/ethnic dynamics that are also present, help to fuel the abuse? In US mass media news, racial/ethnic identity is usually not mentioned if those involved are white.[4] However, even the absence of a racial identification for white victim-survivors, perpetrators, or church communities in accounts of clergy sexual abuse has significance. It reflects the privilege of whiteness in US society, the privilege of not having to think about racial implications. But for primary (abused person) and secondary (pastoral charge/church community of abuser) victim-survivors who are white, could expectations of privilege and entitlement that are so normalized that they are rarely if ever acknowledged or questioned, perhaps intensify feelings of devastation, confusion, shame, or demoralization at being victimized by trusted white clergy members? As mentioned above, a clergy perpetrator's white maleness could be essential in fostering trust in his authority and thus function as part of his arsenal of socio-religious power that intimidates and provokes feelings of powerlessness for those he victimizes. These interconnected emotional, spiritual, and social dynamics of clergy sexual abuse deserve much more in-depth study.

II. Exploring the experience of psychosocial anguish

Specific examples will help to clarify how destructive psychosocial effects can be manifested in the experience of clergy sexual abuse and why their combined impact must be addressed as morally harmful.

Intimidation may be part of the physical brutality of the abuse. For example, as a thirteen-year-old altar boy, Hank Bachmann was repeatedly summoned by his priest James Gummersbach to the basement of a St Louis, Missouri, church where Gummersbach blindfolded him, 'tied his hands to a pipe, stripped him,' and then raped him.[5] How did the maleness of his abuser contribute? That is, how did the physical strength of this man tying him up, the pain and brutality inflicted in the rapes, the fact that the abuser was a male authority figure in the community, and a representative of God the Father, contribute to the intimidation of this boy by his abuser who kept calling him back for repeated assaults? Suing the church about the abuse that occurred when he was a child involved a gruelling court battle for Bachmann, with multiple phases. Finding the final result disappointing, Bachmann commented: 'I feel all of this anger that he was allowed to get away with it, that the church was allowed to get away with it . . . I can't forgive and I can't forget. The thing is, I still feel like I'm responsible for what happened.'[6] The combined psychosocial consequences are clearly evident in this statement. The emotional reaction is inseparable from the institutional betrayal. Furthermore, I wonder how gender issues might help to reinforce this victim-survivor's struggle with self-blame. They might be a factor in that part of the cultural meaning of manhood often communicated to males includes messages about not 'letting' someone brutalize you and that you are responsible for it if you do 'let' someone do that to you. Social messages such as this about maleness, and the lack of institutional accountability (of church and courts), reinscribe the abuser's disdainful torment of the boy.

Intimidation in the experience of clergy sexual abuse can be more disguised than in Bachmann's experience. It can take the form of the coercive element in the perpetrator's manipulation of friendship and trust. A male victim-survivor of Revd Ronald Paquin, from the Boston Archdiocese, had a long-term series of encounters with Paquin over several years. The abuse started when he was an altar boy at age eleven or twelve. This victim-survivor of abuse said that he viewed Pacquin as a father figure because of how gently the emotional relationship was cultivated (alongside the sexual contact). In what was the boy's first sexual experience, he describes how the priest was 'physically bringing me to ejaculation. He was very gentle about it . . . He'd say 'Are you okay? This is completely normal.' He said it was just a good feeling. And that's how he pitched it: it's good to have an ejaculation, it's good to be comfortable with him.'[7]

Gender issues (linked to sexuality) are evident here in the way that this encounter with an older male authority figure teaches the boy about male sexual functioning (orgasms) and in how this abuser 'guides' him through a kind of 'right of passage' into male sexual maturity, his first sexual experience of ejaculation through stimulation by another person. Maleness is at issue in how this victim-survivor also pointed out his sense of being fathered by the priest whom he felt had taught him about right and wrong through repeated, long conversations, and treated him like a son. Intimidation in this instance takes place through continual coercive pressure applied with seeming kindness and gentleness. Moral manipulation is a tool of the abuser that further compounds the moral harm inflicted. This priest, friend, mentor, father figure pressures him to understand this abuse as a good, normal encounter.

Parallel gender issues surface in the situation of a woman who was sexually abused over a period of fifteen years by a priest she identifies as her 'spiritual father'. The pastoral relationship started when she was a senior in high school. Feeling hurt and isolated by the sexual abuse by her biological father, the death of her mother, and the lack of support from her own church community, she sought a church to which she 'had no family or cultural ties'.[8] She explains that she was the only black child in her hometown to get polio and describes the inappropriate touching of her leg by the priest early in their pastoral relationship as she 'told him about being bewildered by my father's touch during my hospitalization with polio'.[9] (Her father's sexual abuse intensified after she came home, especially after her mother's death when she was fourteen.) As she describes the painful memory of her father molesting her while she was in the hospital, the clergy perpetrator exploits her vulnerability, using it as an opportunity for his own abusive behaviour.

She went to this priest, Patrick, for counselling as a college student, uncertain and anxious about experiencing feelings of attraction to a classmate in her 'delayed puberty'. She describes how, 'sitting close to me, he told me I needed to express the sexual feelings in a safe place, with him. He began to kiss me, laughing at my inexperience when I didn't know what to do with his tongue in my mouth. He quieted any opposition with the assertion that he knew what was best for me. During later appointments he showed me things to avoid with boys if I wanted to be a good Christian girl.'[10] The perpetrator intimidates her, coercing her in a belittling manner. Gender issues related to sexuality and her particular biography help to accomplish this intimidation. The boundary confusion and emotional neediness she brought because of the abuse by her father influenced her to seek out a 'spiritual father' who would be trustworthy on matters of sexuality. Also, gendered social and religious messages that teach women to be submissive, especially to male authority, may also aid the abuser's ability to intimidate her.

Later as she works on her recovery, issues of race arise in her therapeutic acknowledgment of her anger about the abuse. She says: 'I seethe as I struggle to understand what trait of mine signalled that I would not challenge his authority. Did my race give him the assurance that my revelation of abuse would be ignored or disbelieved?'[11] The necessity to analyse racial dynamics in her experience of sexual abuse is a socially imposed burden of a racist society that adds to her anguish. It led to an inquiry about if and how something about her own identity gave permission for the abusive treatment she received. Her moral worth – her right be treated with respect and to receive trustworthy pastoral care – is diminished by her (lack of) racial/ gender status.

Issues of race can also be a source of trust the perpetrator can manipulate. A man accused Revd Maurice Blackwell of sexually abusing him in Baltimore Maryland starting at the age of fourteen or fifteen and lasting until he was about twenty-six years old. The man recalled his initial admiration for the priest: 'I was always in awe of him, a real black priest just being himself.'[12] He met Blackwell during the late 1960s, a period of widely publicized support for black nationalism and black power, especially in eastern, urban black communities like Baltimore. With his Afro, dashiki and self-assured attitude, Blackwell was apparently a charismatic role-model, exhibiting black maleness the boy admired. This perpetrator would rescue him from beatings by physically abusive parents and take him to spend the night at his seminary and subsequently in the rectories he was assigned to serve where he sexually abused him with kissing, fondling and oral sex.[13] Psychosocial longings for respect and dignity fed by a racist society as well as abusive parents add to the vulnerability and trauma in this man's experience of clergy sexual abuse.

III. Psychosocial factors in institutional responses

Destructive psychosocial dynamics that are part of incident(s) of clergy sexual abuse and the anguish the abused person suffers are reproduced in community responses.

As in other forms of sexual assault and abuse, in clergy sexual abuse the victimization of females has triggered discussion about degrees of victimization. Are certain instances of clergy sexual abuse morally worse than others because certain victim-survivors of it are more innocent than others? Some church officials see clergy abuse of females as a lesser moral depravity. Chicago's Cardinal Francis George commented that: 'There's a difference between a moral monster like Geoghan who preys upon little children and does so in a serial fashion and someone who, perhaps under the influence of alcohol, engages in an action with a 17 or 16 year old young woman who returns his affection.'[14] [Geoghan was a predator protected by the church while he abused many boys in the Boston Archdiocese.] Similarly, before his resignation Bishop Bernard Law commented during a deposition in a lawsuit against the Boston Archdiocese that 'there was a "qualitative difference" between clergy sexual abuse toward a minor and toward a female. Law's lawyers cut off the questioning before Law could explain the difference . . .'[15] Assertions such as these by church leaders depicting a moral hierarchy for evaluation of clergy sexual abuse, where only boys under twelve are labelled as truly innocent, institutionally reproduces the traumatizing behaviour of abusers. It uses gender as a way of morally devaluing the worth of certain victim-survivors, preying upon their vulnerability (their victimization by clergy), exploiting their lack of power, sadistically maintaining control and authority that serves the interests of the institutionally powerful

Even when females complain about sexual abuse that occurred when they were minors they have not necessarily been taken seriously. For example, when Anguella, now sixty, complained to Oakland California Diocese officials in the early1990s that she had been raped by a priest as an eight-year-old she was subjected to extensive psychological testing. 'Me!' she says, her voice still resonating with disbelief. 'They thought I was the crazy one . . . Maybe I am crazy, but if I am, there's a good reason for it. It's what they put me through.' Nothing, she says, was done to comfort her or to punish the priest.[16] Anguella's situation demonstrates how psychological issues, or more precisely, emotional woundedness is used against the abused person by institutional representatives responding to her complaint.

At the same time, psychological diagnoses have been used to protect and reinstate clergy perpetrators, willingly putting those under their pastoral authority at risk. Father John Calicott who served a five hundred member church in Chicago, was removed in 1994 from his parish after he admitted to committing the 'sexual misconduct' which two men complained had occurred when they were boys under his pastoral care. He was sent for psychiatric treatment and then reinstated in 1995 to his parish duties including teaching at 'the largest African American Catholic grammar school' in the US. In explaining his decision to return Calicott to his pastoral assignment, Archbishop Bernardin reportedly indicated 'doctors had concluded that his behaviour was not "an expression of a fundamental psychological disorder"'. Moreover, Bernardin pointed out that his congregation favoured his return.[17] In a 2002 interview Calicott, an African American, explains: 'I think sometimes that in the black community, because we've been an

oppressed community, there is a greater understanding that we are all
sinners, that people fail, situations are extremely complex.' His reference to
black oppression functions as an insidious appeal to racial group loyalty to
justify acceptance of his behaviour (at the expense of those victimized by his
abuse?). According to Calicott's assertion, if I were a black person he had
abused (or any black person) and I disagreed with him, I would be breaking
with common understandings of 'our community'. I would be refuting our
community's experience of oppression that just happens to justify protecting him from being held accountable with serious consequences for his
violation of trust, abuse of power, and damage to children as a perpetrator of
clergy sexual misconduct. (The black community could be forgiving
towards him if he served a prison term.) Moreover, oppression may have
distorted black people's expectations so that they are accepting and forgiving of mistreatment in self-destructive ways that must be resisted. Callicot's
self-justifying assertion also gives emphasis to the theological notion of forgiveness of sins. He uses his clerical authority as teacher and pastor to align
acceptance of his behaviour without further consequences, with the expression of Christian faith. Issues of racism and the very idea of psychological
disorder are manipulated by institutional leaders to produce a systemic
denial that any significant harm has been done to those abused. As psychiatrist Richard Sipes writes, 'Psychiatry and psychology can be enlisted to
defend a clerical system. The church will not flourish by enlisting profes-
sions to help it avoid basic issues that tolerate and perpetuate abuse.'[18]

There are emancipatory possibilities for victim-survivors of clergy sexual
abuse when psychosocial factors that abet and nurture the abuse are
revealed. Victim-survivors may be able to glimpse some of the ways that
they are 'set up' for anguish by such factors during and after the sexual
abuse. Analysis of that process implicates all of us in the broader society
in the sexual abuse. Our hegemonic understandings of gender and race/
ethnicity, among other social categories that are institutionally supported
and routinized, in practice help to perpetuate clergy sexual abuse, intensifying the trauma of victim-survivors. If that trauma is to be alleviated and
further trauma prevented, solely blaming individual 'sick' clergy perpetrators, homophobic scapegoating, appeals to Christian forgiveness and black
racial unity, ignoring women/blaming women victim-survivors, any attach-
ment of moral authority to maleness – all represent examples of systemic
corruption that will have to be jettisoned in Christian institutional responses to clergy sexual abuse. A socially and institutionally sustained problem
like clergy sexual abuse can be socially and institutionally defused.

Notes

1. Len Sperry, *Sex, Priestly Ministry, and the Church*, Collegeville, MN: Liturgical Press 2003, p. 106.
2. Nanette de Fuentes, 'Hear Our Cries: Victim Survivors of Clergy Sexual Misconduct' in Thomas G. Plante (ed), *Bless Me Father For I Have Sinned: Perspectives on Sexual Abuse Committed by Roman Catholic Priests*, Westport: Praeger 1999, p. 146.
3. For example, see: Sacha Pfeiffer, *Boston Globe*, 'Women face stigma of clergy abuse, many are reluctant to come forward', 27 December 2002, p. A1; Marilyn Elias, 'Is Homosexuality to Blame for the Child Sexual Abuse Crisis Now Plaguing the Catholic Church?; Assumptions persist but study says gays are no more likely than heterosexuals to molest kids', *USA Today* final edition, 16 July 2002, p. D 06.
4. Most news reporters believe that they should racially identify the subjects of their stories only when relevant. But most reporters view whiteness as a 'normal' identity that is intrinsically less relevant (less newsworthy) than identifying racial 'others' who appear in stories. Therefore the privileging of whiteness as norm tends to be maintained.
5. Sandra G. Boodman, ' How Deep the Scars of Abuse? Some Victims Crippled; Others Stay Resilient', *Washington Post*, 29 July 2002, p. A01ff.
6. Ibid.
7. The Investigative Staff of the Boston Globe, *Betrayal: The Crisis in the Catholic Church*, Boston: Little, Brown and Company 2002, p. 63.
8. 'Et Al' (Pseud.), 'Repairing the Damage of a Shepard' in Nancy Werking Poling, *Victim to Survivor: Women Recovering from Clergy Sexual Abuse*, Cleveland Ohio: United Church Press 1999, p. 23.
9. Ibid., p. 25.
10. Ibid., p. 26.
11. Ibid., p. 35.
12. Robert E. Pierre, 'Haunted by Wounds of the Church; Man Describes Abuse by Maryland Priest, Anguish Afterward', *Washington Post*, 3 June 2002, p. A01. Blackwell was shot and wounded by Dontee Stokes in 2002 who was then tried and acquitted for it mainly because of evidence about the abuse. Stokes had previously complained to the Archdiocese of Baltimore about being sexually abused in 1993 but his complaints were not believed and Blackwell was returned to the parish after a three-month suspension. Annie Gowen, 'Priest shooting may not result in Jail time', 18 December 2002, p. B02.
13. Pierre, 'Haunted by Wounds of the Church' (n. 12).
14. Alan Cooperman, '"One Strike" Plan for Ousting Priests Has Catholics Divided', *Washington Post*, 19 May 2002, pp. A01ff. Also see: Kathy Shaw, Thomas Farragher and Matt Carroll, 'Church Board Dismissed Accusations by Females', *Boston Globe*, 7 February 2003; Robin Washington, 'Critics of Vatican say girls forgotten: Ban on gay priests called off the mark', 7 November 2002.

15. Stephen Kurkjian and Sacha Pfeiffer, 'Woman's Alleged Abuse By Priest "Personal", Wrote Law: Alleged Assault "Personal"', *Boston Globe*, 15 August 2002, p. A1.

16. Jennifer Carnig, 'Restoring Faith; Bay Area Clergy sexual abuse survivors work toward mutual healing', *Oakland* Tribune, 28 April 2002, Bay Area Living Section, p. 4.

17. Alan Cooperman, '"One Strike" Plan for Ousting Priests Has Catholics Divided' (n.14).

18. A. Richard Sipes, 'The Problem of Prevention in Clergy Sexual Abuse' in Thomas G. Plante, (ed), *Bless Me Father For I Have Sinned* (n. 2).

II. Theological Approaches: Biblical, Historical, Systematic

Sexual Violence against Children in the Bible

ANDREAS MICHEL

I. Violence

In the biblical texts there is a wide range of passages which have violence as their subject almost incidentally. They include almost 200 texts about violence against children in the Hebrew Old Testament, another 50 from the deutero-canonical writings of the Old Testament, and a few from the New Testament.[1]

The topic of violence against children runs out in the New Testament. That has much to do with Jesus' rejection of physical violence and of his high respect for children. But where the New Testament speaks of events in wars, violence against children is again present in a classical way; compare for example the apocalyptic cry of woe of Jesus over pregnant women and nursing mothers in Mark 13.17 with II Kings 8.12 and Hosea 14.1. However, the key New Testament text, the climax and turning point in respect of violence against children, is the massacre of the children in Bethlehem in Matt. 2.16ff. The negative evaluation of this excess of violence remains a hermeneutical key to the topic of violence and children at the start of the New Testament

Violence against children appears primarily in the context of descriptions or threats of war, usually as brutal and deadly human violence: children become the victims of armed force, cannibalism, imprisonment, slavery and the extermination of dynasties. The texts about the slaughter of the

Egyptian firstborn and the widespread phenomenon of child sacrifice also relate to the image of God. Social, parental and structural violence is attested in the practice of exposing newborn girl babies; it can be found in the framework of slavery for debt; in the case of fatherless orphans; and, for modern sensibilities, also in rough practices of upbringing. In this overall situation of life-threatening violence against children, which reflects social realities at the time when the texts were written, sexual violence against children plays more of a marginal role.

II. Children

This verdict also depends on the definition of what we understand by 'child' in the biblical, and especially in the ancient Near Eastern, context, and how we identify 'children' in the Bible.[2]

In terms of vocabulary alone it is difficult to define the age of those concerned: only examples using words like 'infant' or 'suckling' are clear. All other words for child contain ambivalences: 1. They sometimes also appear as a designation for descent, in which case they denote the sequence of generations ('son', 'daughter', 'descendant'). 2. They are not age-specific and can certainly denote young people, even adults ('child', 'boy', 'girl'). 3. They are predominantly terms in social law ('young woman', 'girl'). One example is Amos 2.7, which complains bitterly that 'a man and his father go to the same girl (na'^{e}ra)', i.e. have sexual intercourse with her. However, here the thought is not of the abuse of a girl before the age of puberty; 'girl (na'^{e}ra)' is probably the term in social law for an independent woman of indeterminate age who is a member of the family.[3]

In terms of social history we are moving in a milieu before the modern discovery of childhood.[4] The attempt to apply to the Bible the concept of childhood or youth which has been coined in modern times has anachronistic, if not cultural-colonialist features: in an agrarian culture, in which dwelling-place and work are hardly separate, in which phases of learning and education outside the family are little known, and in which therefore children are integrated into the family process of production at a very early stage, before puberty, childhood does not look the same as it does in the well-to-do modern Northern hemisphere today. It is questionable how far we can speak of 'youth' at all where, particularly in the case of girls, marriagable age in practice begins with puberty, and in the case of unmarried girls dependence on the father under social law can also extend far beyond the age of eighteen, which is so significant today.

III. Sexual violence against children and abuse

The words 'sex' or 'sexual' do not appear in German translations of the Bible. The now much-used term 'abuse' has no place in passages about sexual matters in the Luther Bible, and in the modern ecumenical translation it appears only in Judg. 19.25; Ezek. 16.15, 25; 22.10, 11. A search for the polyvalent word 'abuse' or 'abuser' in English or French translations produces almost grotesque results. In Luke 6.28 the Revised Standard Version calls on its readers to 'bless those who curse you, pray for those who abuse you'. The French ecumenical translation even presents the God YHWH as an 'abuser' of his people: '*Seigneur Dieu, assurément tu as bien abusé ce people et Jérusalem*' (Jer. 4.10)'; however, the following '*en disant*' explains that this is merely verbal abuse (Jer. 20.7 is comparable).

A look at all three words in the title of this article, 'violence', 'children' and 'sexual (abuse)' suggests the need for caution in exploring cases and calls for critical reflection on what sometimes may be anachronistic judgments. It is important to investigate the translations so that they do not create problems – as in the example of Luke 6.28 mentioned above – which are not in the original text. As well as asking 'Is the text speaking of children at all?', we must also consider whether we simply have phenomena of social history which pass almost uncommented on in the text. Are value judgments being made in the context of the account? Is the possibly negative evaluation in line with our present-day perspective, or do quite different perspectives emerge?

IV. Sexual abuse of boys?

Sexual violence against boys or young men certainly occurs in I Macc. 2.46, in the expressly (!) violent compulsory circumcision of the male children of Israel under Mattathias, the father of the Maccabee brothers; here, however, we should certainly not speak of sexual abuse but of religious violence.

Sexual activities with male children can be recognized in I Cor. 6.9, where there is polemic against *malakoi*, 'weaklings',[5] a word which points to the sphere of the phenomenon of Greek pederasty.[6] However the context – and also the following *arsenoko/tai* (men having sexual relations with men) – does not suggest that the conduct or action hinted at by the 'weaklings' has been associated with physical force or even psychological force.[7]

The ancient Near East does not present a uniform picture of pederasty, and in contrast to the Greek sphere this picture is only schematic. The best preserved ancient Babylonian 'love dialogue' (end of the third millennium to at the latest the middle of the second millennium) can say uninhibitedly:

'Grant me honour, flattery and constant contact with my boy' (TUAT II, 5, 744). If the translation, which is disputed, is correct, by contrast the Egyptian Teaching of Ptahotep (end of the third millennium) speaks of pederastic practices: 'Do not sleep with an attractive boy, you do not know how to resist the seed from his member' (TUAT II, 2,213). Hittite law (middle of the second millennium) maintains: 'If a man sins with his (a) son, (that is) a misdeed' (TUAT I, 1, 122).

Granted, texts on pederasty occur only sporadically in the ancient Near East; nevertheless it is striking that there is no prohibition against pederasty in the Old Testament. So far – and rightly – it has not been concluded from this lack that pederasty was usual and permitted in ancient Israel. However, the weight of the evidence seems to be quite different in the discussion of the lack of a prohibition against incest with one's daughter in Lev. 18.

Moreover – as in the ancient Near East – there is evidence of the prostitution of both males and females in Israel. That is particularly clear in Deut. 23.18, which speaks of 'the hire of a harlot' and 'the wages of a dog'.[8] Whether and how far commercial relations of a pederastic kind were included here[9] can no longer be determined, given the sparsity of Old Testament sources. Historically speaking it is questionable whether the term 'sacred initiates' in Deut. 23.17; I Kings 14.22; 15.12; 22.47; II Kings 23.7; Hos. 4.14 refers to sexual, even cultic practices; at any rate it is unclear how these relate to 'children'. The 'pleasure boys' in the German ecumenical translation of Job 36.14 is also a disputed rendering.[10] However we interpret the biblical references to boys/young men, in the context such behaviour is regularly disapproved of; nevertheless, there is no mention of violence.

Granted, there is mention in Gen. 39 of violence and an attempt at abuse, of which the narrator disapproves (!), of the slave Joseph by Potiphar's wife. But Gen. 39.4 already says: 'He [Potiphar] appointed him [Joseph] steward of his house and entrusted all his possessions to him'; here we are hardly to imagine a 'youthful Joseph'.[11] However, only the social difference between slave and mistress and of course the difference in sex plays a role in the text.

V. Sexual abuse of girls: rape

No biblical text deals explicitly with sexual activities with girls below the age of puberty. All the texts in which female figures are abused, usually raped, even suggest the opposite, without stating it in so many words. The texts or their authors are not interested in the question of age, most probably because they simply presuppose the sexual maturity of the girl or young woman mentioned as the norm. Moreover in almost all such texts the technical term *bᵉtul* is used. This denotes a young woman who is sexually mature, but in social law is still dependent on her father.[12] Such *bᵉtul* texts which are relevant for us occur in Ex. 22.15–16; Deut. 22.23–29; Judg. 19.24; II Sam. 13.2; I Kings 1.2; Esther 2.2–3 and Lam. 5.11. None of these biblical texts is interested in the specific age of the women concerned, but only in their legal and social status, and above all in whether the woman is still subject to her father or husband. To take an example: for the text, the author and the intended reader of II Sam. 17 it makes no difference whether the half-sister Tamar, who has been raped and abused, and who is called *bᵉtul*, is fourteen or twenty-four. All that is relevant is that Amnon has intervened violently in his father's sphere of power, which extends to his unmarried daughter Tamar.

Nevertheless it is possible – and here things are better than in Gen. 34 (the rape of Dinah) – to understand II Sam. 13 as a narrative about the abuse of a minor. The constellation of perpetrator, victim and constellation fits abuse: Amnon comes from the close social, family environment. Moreover Absalom's instructions to Tamar to keep quiet (v. 20) also fit in with this: 'Do not say anything about it, my sister, he is your brother.' Moreover here the victim in her status (as sister) is firmly put under the two (!) brothers, and in this way additionally victimized. Nevertheless, although maintaining patriarchal categories throughout, the narrative clearly disapproves of Tamar's rape or abuse and puts Tamar as victim at the centre of the reader's empathy. Indeed Amnon's action even justifies his murder, which is depicted next (II Sam. 13.32).

Rape and the abuse of minors in the modern sense which that perhaps also includes is punished in the legal regulations of Deut. 22.23–39. Here – in contrast to Ex. 22.15–16 – the Deuteronomistic regulation Deut. 22.28–29 emphasizes the absence of consent on the part of the young woman (*bᵉtul*) and thus the violent character of the action. In the chaos of the post-war period Lam. 5.11 complains of the rape of 'young women in the cities of Judah', which may also have included 'minors'. However, these events are – rightly – complained of to God.

What are not complained about are 'lesser' forms of sexual violence of the kind which occur in I Kings 1.1–4 and Esther 2. The sexual violence which occurs there is limited or legitimated by relationships resembling marriage. That in Esther 2 'young women' become victims of sexual or sexualized violence is not made a specific theme; it is never claimed, let alone disapproved of. No questions are asked about the willingness of the women concerned. However, Esther 2 with its legendary features is not too far removed from a modern Miss World contest.

More serious than II Sam. 13 is the text of Judg. 19 (with the use of the designation *b*ᵉ*tul*) and then Gen. 19, where the designation *b*ᵉ*tul* is absent: in Gen. 19 we find only the negative statement that the two daughters of Lot 'have not known a man'; we are told nothing of their age. If we read Gen. 19 in the light of Judg. 19, then the young women here may likewise be beyond the age of puberty. The narrator also allows virtually no time to elapse between the episodic stay in Zoar in Gen. 19.30 and the narrative in Gen. 19.30–38, which presents the two daughters as being of an age to bear children. Consequently Lot is not offering the aggressive people of Sodom the opportunity to abuse girls below the age of puberty, even if it is conceded that this differentiation reflects our question rather than that of the text, author and intended reader. To this degree, while comparable with II Sam. 13, Judg. 19 and Gen. 19 are more clumsy in their ethical and moral message: the daughters in both Gen. 19 and Judg. 19 are under the heedless rule of their father, who in weighing up the balance between hospitality and the virginity of the girl which he himself (!) has put in question decides for the male guest (in Judg. 19 only for the male guest) and against his daughters. In both cases what we then have is not the abuse of the daughter or daughters but the gang rape of the Levite's concubine in Judg. 19 (is she fully of age in the modern sense?). Moreover the two texts Gen. 19 and Judg.19 are not concerned with the subjective side of the (potential) female victims (II Sam. 13 differs). At all events it is clear that the offer of a daughter or daughters is an evil, even if it is a lesser evil than the violation of the law of hospitality.

In a hermeneutic of suspicion we can also read the whole of Gen. 19 through the spectacles of incestuous abuse by the father: Lot, who understands his daughters virtually as possessions and therefore makes them sexually available (29.7), drives them into outward isolation (19.30). The androcentric narrator foists the father's wish for sexual contact on to his daughters as the ones who cause it (29.31).[13] Such a view certainly fails to recognize the narrator's intention in Gen. 19, but it does make us sensitive to bad influence which such texts exert: Genesis 19 has in fact been used as a religious legitimation by fathers who have abused their daughters.[14]

VI. Abduction of girls, slavery, servitude for debt: abuse of dependents?

In a quite unique way, in the context of the Midianite war Num. 31.18 remarks: 'But all the following under the women who have not known man by lying with him, keep alive for yourselves.' The term 'following under the women' means 'children – and probably the young (in the sense of a *b*ᵉ*tul*) under the women', i.e. girls in the wider sense (cf. also Num. 31.9). Above all, in a horrifying way there is no limitation of age in the direction of small children. The lack of such a limitation, the clear sexual connotations ('who have not known man'), together with the 'for you', and additionally the fact that this is a positive instruction or permission given by Moses characterize the verse in the context of sexual violence against children as markedly harsh. Granted, we can console ourselves with the fact that this way of dealing with the victims itself represents the lesser evil: it means that they are spared the massacre suffered by the men, the women who are no longer virgins and the male children and young. Nevertheless the 'what for' and 'when' in the sense of the age of the girls remains intolerably obscure.[15] There is a milder formulation in the narrative of the war and abduction of women in Judg. 21: first of all there is mention of 'young women' (*b^etul*) in connection with the campaign against Jabesh-gilead (Judg. 21.12). Secondly it is clear, as also in the abduction of women in Shiloh, that the abducted women are really to take the status of wives (Judg. 21.7, 14, 16, 18). The brief biblical notes on the plundering, abduction and enslavement of 'women and children' and so on could thus imply sexual violence, even if this is not explicitly mentioned.[16] Deuteronomy 21.10–14 introduces a humanization within Israel, the rule that a prisoner of war should be married. II Kings 5 (here 5.2 and the whole context) shows that the fate of a young (!) girl who is abducted could also be free of (narrated) sexual violence.

Exodus 21.7–11 stands for a similar humanizing of the fate of women sold into slavery for debt; here sexual intercourse is even depicted as a legal claim and not as a threat to the slave, together with food and clothing (cf. Ex. 2.10). Nehemiah 5.5 has another tone; it is often understood to mean that some of the enslaved 'daughters' have already become victims of sexual violence. However, the logic of the text must be different. What is meant is that the economic situation is so difficult that 'we are forcing our sons and our daughters to be slaves, and some of our daughters have already been enslaved'. In that case the difference between the two halves of the statement is not between sale and abuse but between the threat of having to sell all one's children and the sale of a few of them which has already taken place, who are only daughters (!); here the passive formulation of the second clause is silent about the role of the parents. Sexual connotations are not to the fore in Neh. 5.5; in any case nothing is said about the age of the 'daughters'.[17]

VII. Incest with one's own daughter?

In the Old Testament the discussion of abuse is carried on in particular over the lack of a prohibition of incest with a daughter in Lev. 18.7–16.[18]

The prohibition does not occur in all the collections of ancient Near Eastern law but only in the Codex Hammurabi, §154: 'If a citizen knows his daughter (sexually) this citizen shall be drivn out of the city' (TUAT I, 1, p. 61) and in the Hittite Law, §189: 'If a man sins with his own mother (it is) a misdeed. If a man sins with his (a) daughter, (it is) a misdeed. If a man sins with his (a) son, (it is) a misdeed' (TUAT I, 1, pp. 121f.).[19]

Above, I argued at length that the explicit lack of such a prohibition in the Old Testament does not simply allow us to conclude that incest between father and daughter was permitted.[20] In any case, in Lev. 18 at least young women, and not children, are meant. Otherwise it seems to me most plausible that Lev. 18.7–16 does not mention the daughters because this catalogue is about the violation of the legal claims of other males. There is no place of a prohibition against incest with one's own daughter here; the case is different with a granddaughter (hence Lev. 18.10). Moreover the catalogue of incest in 18.7–16 is framed by the two norms of Lev. 18.6 and Lev. 18.17a. As a kind of basic norm, however, Lev. 18.6 also prohibits sexual contact with a daughter (cf. Lev. 18.6 with Lev. 21.2!). Leviticus 18.7a explicitly prohibits intercourse with a woman and her daughter; moreover it is not, as in the case of v.18, limited to the lifetime of the woman (cf. also Lev. 20.14). The canonical text is thus sufficiently clear in condemning incest with a daughter. By contrast one can only speculate about the preliminary literary stages of the incest catalogue, possibly the omission of a prohibition of incest with a daughter and the reasons for it.

Moreover at the level of the Pentateuch Deut. 22.13–21 has to be set alongside Lev. 18. The shame that a woman does not come to marriage as a virgin falls back on the 'father's house' (v. 21). But the stones that bring death hit only the daughters!

VIII. Conclusion

The anachronism of looking at the Bible in terms of violence and children can hardly be avoided. The perception of children as subjects at law and subjects of their own development is largely lacking in the Bible, nor does it know the concept of individual rights to protection. There is no evidence of sexual violence against children below the age of puberty – unless it is perhaps implied in Num. 31.17. Sexual violence against young woman above the age of puberty is largely disapproved of or depicted as an evil, but essentially in the interest of the men concerned, especially the father. To this degree women victims can be victimized twice (Deut. 22.21), but there are also the beginnings of sympathy for the victim (II Sam. 13). The Bible remains cautious in its formulations and is in no way interested in excessive description. Sexual violence against children remains at the level of human violence, and in conclusion it must be stated quite emphatically that in no case is God depicted as an abuser of children.

Translated by John Bowden

Notes

1. Cf. Andreas Michel, *Gott und Gewalt gegen Kinder im Alten Testament*, FAT 37, Tübingen 2003, pp. 31–65.
2. For the vocabulary of childhood especially in the Hebrew Old Testament see ibid., pp. 21–7.
3. See Jörg Jeremias, *Der Prophet Amos* (ATD 24,2), Göttingen 1995, pp. 22–3.
4. The basic study is Philippe Ariès, *Centuries of Childhood. A History of Family Life*, New York 1962.
5. For this text cf. Frank-Lothar Hossfeld, 'Gottes Heiligkeit und die Sexualität des Menschen – alttestamentliche Hintergründe zur Position des Paulus in 1 Kor 5–7' in Marlis Gielen and Joachim Kügler (eds), *Liebe, Macht und Religion. Interdisziplinäre Studien zu Grunddimensionen menschlicher Existenz, Gedenkschrift für Helmut Merklein*, Stuttgart 2003, pp.83–95: 84ff.
6. For pederasty in ancient Greece (with 12–18 year olds, not boys), see *Der Neue Pauly* 9, 2000, cols 39–141 s.v. 'Päderastie'.
7. Cf. Hossfeld, 'Gottes Heiligkeit' (n. 5), p. 85, n. 9. The usual harsh German translation of *arsenokoitai* as '*Knabenschänder*' ('those who sexually violate boys', also I Tim 1.10) is unjustified; the English translations rightly think of more generael homosexual practices.
8. For the interpretation of Deut. 28.(18–)19 cf. Christian Frevel, *Aschera und der Ausschließlichkeitsanspruch YHWHs. Beiträge zu literarischen, religionsgeschichtlichen und ikonographischen Aspekten der Ascheradiskussion* (2 vols), BBB 94, Weinheim 1995, pp. 643ff, esp. pp. 647–8.
9. For the whole phenomenon of homosexuality see Martti Nissinen, *Homoeroticism in the Biblical World. A Historical Perspective*, Minneapolis 1998, and more generally Volkert Haas, *Babylonischer Liebesgarten. Erotik und Sexualität im Alten Orient*, Munich 1999.
10. For Job 36.14 cf. Frevel, *Aschera* (n. 8), pp. 709f.
11. Against Irmtraud fischer, 'Über Lust und Last, Kinder zu haben. Soziale, genealogische und theologische Aspekte in der Literatur Alt-Israels', *JBT* 17, 2002, pp. 55–82: 63.
12. Cf. Ilse Müllner, *Gewalt im Hause Davids. Die Erzählung von Tamar und Amnon (2Sam 13,1–22)*, HBS 13, Freiburg etc. 1997, pp.203–5.

13. Cf. Elke Seifert, *Tochter und Vater im Alten Testament. Eine ideologiekritische Untersuchung zur Verfügungsgewalt von Vätern über ihre Töchter*, Neukirchener Theologische Dissertationen und Habilitationen 9, Neukirchen-Vluyn 1997, pp. 82–6, 175–8, 184–5.

14. There is a similar testimony e.g. in Carol A. J. Adams et al. (eds), *Violence against Women and Children. A Christian Theological Sourcebook*, New York 1995.

15. Martin Noth, *Numbers*, OTL, London and Philadelphia 1966, ad loc., takes the milder view that the Midianite women are to be 'concubines' and slaves'. But if there are no sexual connotations one also asks oneself why the young Midianite boys could not also have been made slaves.

16. Cf. especially in Gen. 34.29; Num. 14.3,31; 31.9; Deut. 1.39; 20.14; 28.32, 41; I Sam. 30.2, 3,19; Jer. 6.11; II Chron. 28.8; 29.9; I Macc. 1.32; 5.13; 8.10; II Macc. 5.14, 24; Judith 4.12; 16.4.

17. For further texts on the enslavement of children for debt cf. especially II Kings 4.1; Joel 4.3 (!); Micah 2.9.

18. Cf. e.g. Friedrich Fechter, *Die Familie in der Nachexilszeit. Untersuchungen zur Bedeutung der Verwandtschaft in ausgewählten Texten des Alten Testaments*, BZAW 264, Berlin and New York 1998, pp. 177–87.

19. For incest in the ancient Near East cf. especially Sophie Lafont, *Femmes, Droit et Justice dans l'Antiquité Orientale. Contribution à l'étude du droit pénal au Proche-Orient ancient*, OBO 165, Fribourg and Göttingen 1999, pp.173–236.

20. Lafont, *Femmes* (n.19), 18, differs: 'It follows that cases which are not prohibited by law are regarded as licit.'

Sexual Violence against Children: A Violation of the Protection of Children Grounded in Christianity

HUBERTUS LUTTERBACH

A religious institution like the church, which makes a high moral claim, particularly in the sphere of sexuality, should not be surprised if it comes under especially vigorous attack over sexual transgressions in its own ranks. It is incomprehensible that a priest should commit such a transgression. With these words the Catholic pastoral psychologist Wunibald Muller, who is professionally involved in dealing with priests in crisis situations, puts the abuse of children by pastors in the wider context of physical and psychological violence against children.[1]

More than ever before, over the last two years the Roman Catholic Church has hit the headlines because priests in its ranks who are committing or have committed sexual offences against children in the course of their pastoral activities are still engaged in pastoral duties. In the USA hundreds of priests and religious are being criticized for this, and have been subject to investigations or legal proceedings; such developments have led even to the resignation of bishops.

The urgency of this problem is highlighted by the fact that Pope John Paul II expressed his deep pain over this use of violence immediately after the charges were published and condemned the perpetrators with impressive words. 'The abuse of children is the symptom of a severe crisis which affects not only the church but society as a whole. This is a deep-seated crisis of sexual morality, indeed of human relationships and the principles behind them. The family and children are its victims.' And he went on to speak in quite specific terms of the sexual transgressions within the American clergy: 'People should know that there is no place in the priesthood or in religious orders for those who harm children (sexually). They must know that bishops and priests are utterly committed to the fullness of Christian truth with respect to sexual morality, a truth which is as decisive for the renewal of the priesthood as it is for the renewal of marriage and family life.'[2]

Remarkably, to the present day[3] the focus of such statements by the church and their echo in the media is primarily on particular cases of child abuse. No one ever asks from a historical perspective what role the protection of children from sexual violence has really played in past centuries.[4] This perspective, which is also absent from the gathering of North American bishops who met in the Vatican in June 2002 (and largely also from the resolutions of the German Episcopal Conference) is decisive, because in retrospect the protection of children from sexual interference is to be seen as one of the great humanizing achievements of Christianity. In other words, the social consensus that in principle sexual violence may not be inflicted on children is rooted in the beginnings of Christianity. To this degree the loss of credibility for Christianity is proving all the more serious when Christians and even those closely involved in the work of the church scorn this tradition. I shall be outlining it here. To begin with we must ask how sexual contacts with children were evaluated in ancient Greece and ancient Rome, for only against this background is it possible to demonstrate and explain what a deep change in the history of civilization is marked by the Christian prohibition of sexual attacks on children.

I. Sexual intercourse with children in antiquity

Current talk of paedophilia with a sexual element or pederasty runs the risk of projecting present-day plausibilities back on to history under the influence of the current attitudes. In order to avoid this danger, to begin with it has to be stressed that in ancient Greece pederasty was not understood to be the sexual contact of an adult with small children; rather, the love of a boy by an adult and free man could relate only to a young member of the same class in the closing phase of his existence as a child (Greek *pais*), in other words to a boy between the ages of twelve and eighteen, who moreover like a child was still in a dependent social relationship. The boy would not respond with sexual initiatives to the love of the older man, which was also expressed actively and genitally but might never amount to penetration; at least ideally he remained sexually uninvolved,[5] in order to ground his affection solely on the exemplary citizenship of the older person, whom he sought to imitate.[6]

Secondly, pederasty must not simply be confused with an unbridled expression of sexuality towards boys:[7] 'Sexual restraint was the ideal required by ethics, at least in the late classical period. Granted, in the love of women affection and harmony were also regarded as the model for the framework of marriage, but they were not the essential presupposition. By contrast, the love of boys was based on a human-moral concern for one another, which after an initial phase of pederasty led to lifelong philia (*friendship*).'[8] Beyond doubt a high ethical ideal stood in the background of this friendship of a man with a boy, which was also grounded in sex.[9]

Thirdly, the 'pedagogical eros'[10] in play in the sexual friendship between men and boys meant that the love of boys played a decisive role in the framework of bringing up young men to be good citizens; in the aristocratic society of antiquity, which as yet did not have a public school system but only 'private teachers', the adult was to teach his lover, whom he usually got to know during training in the sports arena (*paleastra*), ideals of behaviour and at the same time to convey civic values.[11] In this sense of furthering society the love of boys could also rise to become an important theme in poetry, and it was expressed iconographically on vases.[12]

Fourthly, in contrast to modern times, in ancient Greece recourse to pederasty was not understood as the expression of an individual disposition: 'The parallel drawn between marital love and the love of boys shows that both stood side by side in the social system of values and were equally accepted. The love of boys as a homo-erotic mode of behaviour was by no means taboo; it was nothing to be ashamed of or to keep hidden . . . The choice of one love or the other was not a matter of individual conditioning but a social convention, dependent on age and social status.'[13]

Since the population structure in ancient Greece meant that there were far more older men than boys between the ages of twelve and eighteen, the men had to woo their young lovers. They mostly sought to win boys over by presents or gifts of money and to assert themselves against rival wooers. Here the love of boys could move into an ethical 'grey zone': 'The love of boys came dangerously near to commercial love, to prostitution.'[14] At any rate in ancient Rome, a pederastic relationship in which the older person was concerned only for his own sexual pleasure and not the boy's upbringing was usually regarded as 'dishonourable and as sexual abuse'.[15] A complicating factor was that from a purely external aspect a pederastic relationship was hardly distinguishable from prostitution, since the intention to educate which was essential to it hardly appeared publicly.[16] Generally speaking, in the ancient world prostitution had a different status from prostitution today: 'Its extent and its social status went far beyond what present-day conditions suggest.'[17] Time and again girls worked as prostitutes, especially if they had been sold in slave markets or exposed by their parents; being an orphan could favour prostitution.[18] According to the ancient historian Bettina Stumpff, the sources speak of parents 'handing over their children for prostitution – and given that homosexual prostitution was widespread this also included boys – or selling them to a pimp'.[19] Here the dire economic

circumstances of parents may have played a decisive role: 'Illiterate prostitutes were so to speak predestined to involve their daughters . . . [in
prostitution] because with their illiteracy they otherwise had few openings
on the labour market, but could instruct their protégés in the trade.'[20] When
Roman authors sometimes put the prostitution of children on the same level
as treason and castration, these condemnations apply only to free citizens; by
contrast slave boys and girls often provided their services in boys' and girls'
brothels which were established specially for them.[21] The legal reaction to
such practices came about 'only in late antiquity', when 'legislation with a
Christian motivation' was enacted, though from the imperial side at least
giving away one's own children was prohibited with the threat of punishment.[22]

II. The prohibition of sexual violence against children in the early church

From the time of the primitive church Christians gave various reasons for
not violating children sexually in any way. A fundamental element in
Christian history is the expectation of the return of Christ, the conviction
that this would take place soon.[23] In view of this return of the Lord which
was thought to be just round the corner, any expression of sexuality was
superfluous for Christians in their all-decisive preparation for the kingdom
of heaven.

Secondly, the Christian renunciation of sex, grounded in the second
coming, meant that the *christianoi*, the adherents of the new way, felt that
they were a 'contrast society' within Roman society. Peter Brown has inves-
tigated in depth the connection between the body and society,[24] i.e. the
relationship between Christians and their bodies on the one hand and
Roman society on the other. Christians refused to allow their bodies to be
taken into service by the pagan, Roman state. Thus from the perspective of
the Roman empire it can be said that: 'Like society, the body was there to be
administered, not to be changed.'[25] Christians firmly dissociated themselves
from this perspective – with far-reaching consequence also for sexual dealings with children which hitherto had been taken for granted: 'Sexual
renunciation might lead the Christian to transform the body and, in trans-
forming the body, to break with the discreet discipline of the ancient city.'[26]
Against this background we can also understand the voices in the early
church which spoke out vigorously against the kidnapping of exposed
children in order to protect them from a career in the brothel which in antiquity was otherwise probable;[27] not least the slavery that threatened exposed

children was often the subject of vigorous protest,[28]especially since prostitution as an expression of sexual exploitation and slavery in the sense of an exploitation of labour often went hand in hand. In both cases people saw children almost certainly delivered over to 'organized kidnapping by robbers, cheats and especially pirates'.[29]

Thirdly, the Christian ideal of avoiding the passions of sexuality among other things linked up with the philosophical convictions of the Greek Stoa. Whereas this philosophical trend had tolerated pederasty, at least in the beginning,[30] Christians from the start allowed the exercise of sexuality only within marriage and merely for the sake of procreation: Paul attacks same-sex sexual relations[31] and prostitution[32] without making sexual dealings with children an explicit topic in this connection.

The fourth all-decisive reason for the Christian disapproval of sexual intercourse with children lies in the great commandment to love God and neighbour: linking up with the ideal of the Stoics who were free from the passions that disturb the spirit, the 'ascetic training' of the Christians of the early church also aimed at initiation into love of God and love of neighbour, as this was shown – in a way unique in the world of the time – especially in care of the weakest members of society. The Christian valuing of children was grounded primarily in the way in which Jesus presented the little ones to adults as models for being children of God (Matt.18.3 par.). Here to some degree he elevated them to a 'holy status'. A further emphatic indication of this is that children are the only group to be shown a 'threefold gesture': laying on of hands, embracing and blessing (Mark 10.15–16). Thus Christian Gnilka rightly speaks in retrospect of a 'new evaluation of being a child',[33] grounded n the Bible, an understanding which never tolerated sexual contacts.

III. Christian repudiation of sexual contacts with children in the Middle Ages

In a slow move away from the ethics of the early church which saw the 'pure heart' guaranteed above all by a committed observance of the New Testament commandment to love, in the early Middle Ages the plausibility of ethical purity shifted to a concern for a guarantee of cultic purity – a prime element in the history of religion. In the light of this taboo-laden notion, which became dominant in Christian history for the first time in this period, it was held from then on that any sexual contact 'profaned' and polluted sacred actions. Mayke de Jong speaks of a 'moral system driven by pollution' as a basic social and religious datum of the Middle Ages.[34] We have to ask how this change, which was also significant for the prohibition of sexual contacts with children, is to be explained.

The key notion of outward cultic impurity which was overcome in the New Testament through links with philosophical and prophetic traditions – in the Old Testament it is to be found predominantly in the Holiness Code (Lev. 18) – gained new influence from the fifth century on under the changed conditions in the Roman empire; for in contrast to the elaborated tradition of ethical purity, the ideal of cultic purity was familiar to the illiterate peoples who thronged into the Western Roman empire from their own traditions.[35] Amazingly, the primacy of cultic purity, which had thus once again become influential after the early Middle Ages, could guarantee the protection of children from sexual attacks as effectively as the concern for the inner purity of the heart which was still normative in the early church: anyone who had sexual dealings with children sinned on the basis of contact with blood and sperm, polluting both himself and his sexual partner. The mediaevalist Heinz Wilhelm Schwarz has constructed a typology of the relevant precepts for protecting children from the sexual attacks of adults by means of church law and secular law in the Middle Ages: 'The quantity and quality of the relevant legal norms of both church and secular authority suggest a lively interest by early medieval society in protecting the child from the delicts mentioned.'[36] From this perspective he emphasizes at another point what is even a special element in the church's influence on these protective regulations in favour of children by comparison with secular law.[37] Over and above the legal precepts, in connection with the protection of children reference can also be made to the mediaeval regulations for religious orders. In them the protection of children in monasteries from sexual interference because of the cultic impurities associated with such actions is virtually a core concern.[38] At any rate from the time of the early church it was customary to accept children in monasteries – a practice which was to last until the high Middle Ages.

IV. The protection of children from sexual interference between the Middle Ages and modernity

The ethics of the early church and the early Middle Ages provided the two reasons why sexual interference with children was always ruled out for Christians. These were: on the one hand the exercise of sexuality for the purpose of procreation which was allowed solely within marriage, and the exemplary character, indeed the holiness, of children which was normatively advocated by Jesus; on the other hand the taboo over blood which rejected any kind of sexuality, including sexual involvement with children, for the sake of observing cultic purity. Indeed these two reasons run through church and secular legislation to the present day. So it may be right to say that while since the eighteenth century the view of intercourse outside marriage as a punishable offence has declined,[39] at the same time children have come to be seen as human beings who are no longer regarded as small adults but as beings at a stage of existence in which they have their own rights. For this reason they have been granted a special degree of protection – not least from sexual interference.[40] This status of the child, which since the eighteenth century has been regarded as 'unique', already had its beginnings in the fifteenth century in interpretations of Jesus' encounter with children; however, it came to exercise a broad influence in society only with the help of the Enlightenment – extending to the 'deification' of the child in Romanticism. Even if since the eighteenth century sexual intercourse outside marriage is said increasingly to have lost the stain of being a 'sin against God', the strict condemnation of acts involving incest and other forms of sexual interference with children by adults have remained. In the nineteenth century the women's movement in particular took on the protection of children. Thus 'new offences were formulated in the sphere of fornication with children and young people which involved the abuse of dependent relationships or teacher-pupil relations; these incurred their own punishments in the houses of discipline, prisons and workhouses which had become customary in the realm of crimes against morality'.[41] Since in the eighteenth and nineteenth centuries education was regarded as a 'sacred' activity involving children who were now regarded as 'holy' and part of 'God's paradise',[42] the notion of protecting children and young people came more and more into public awareness.[43] Even if state legislation today has moved away from the premise that in accordance with the moral teaching of the church men and women have to be presented with the alternative of 'marriage or continence', state and church legislation largely agree in the punishment of sexual interference with children by adults, inside or outside family relationship. Thus what was originally a genuinely Christian concern for the protection of children now resounds not only in church law[44] and the laws of nation states,[45] but also in legal regulations which apply all over the world.

V. Prospects

It is the main concern of the UN Convention on the Rights of the Child to guarantee the protection of children which was initiated by Christianity. In its section 34, this 1989 agreement, which is an important factor all over the world, also calls for the protection of children from sexual interference by adults:

> States Parties undertake to protect the child from all forms of sexual exploitation and sexual abuse. For these purposes, States Parties shall in particular take all appropriate national, bilateral and multilateral measures to prevent:
>
> (a) The inducement or coercion of a child to engage in any unlawful sexual activity;
>
> (b) The exploitative use of children in prostitution or other unlawful sexual practices;
>
> (c) The exploitative use of children in pornographic performances and materials.[46]

Reinhard Jung puts it even more vividly when he translates this article 'into the language of the people for whom this convention is intended'.

> Governments commit themselves to protect children from all forms of sexual abuse and sexual exploitation. Laws and every means are to prevent adults from making the tender and cuddly nature of children a disgusting business. Children must not be compelled to cuddle adults. Children must not be hired out to revolting men to fondle them. Children must not be shown in pornographic literature or films. Children have a right not to have their modesty violated.[47]

To conclude: like all such delicts by lay people, the sexual attacks by Roman Catholic priests on children in the USA (and in Europe) which have recently been publicized threaten to weaken the genuine Christian tradition of the protection of children. If this process of erosion is to be stopped, the events mentioned require the church authorities to expose such cases with the emphasis practised and commended by John Paul II. Secondly, American politicians could ask themselves whether the USA should not sign the convention on the rights of the child as quickly as possible, since in the meantime all states have taken this step with the exception of the USA and Somalia. For both the Roman Catholic Church and for the USA as a new world originally inclined towards the Christian God of peace, this is a matter of their preserving a high degree of credibility in their support of human rights, indeed the clearest and loudest voice on behalf of children in need of protection.[48]

Translated by John Bowden

Notes

1. Wunibald Müller, 'Sexueller Missbrauch Minderjähriger in der Kirche. Pastoraltheologische und pastoralpsychologische Aspekte und Konsequenzen' in Stephen J. Rossetti and Wunibald Müller (eds), *Sexueller Missbrauch Minderjähriger in der Kirche. Psychologische, seelsorgliche und institutionelle Aspekte*, Mainz 1996, pp. 173–94: p. 173.
2. http://www.vatican.va/roman_curia/cardinals/documents/rc_cardinals 20020424_fina.. 29 April 2002.
3. Verena Mosen, 'Verschweigen, Verleugnen, Vertuschen. Die Behinderung der UN-Kinderrechtskonvention durch das katholische Kirchenrecht bei sexuellem Missbrauch von Kindern', *Frankfurter Rundschau*, 6 January 2004, p. 9.
4. For the Christian tradition of the protection of children see my comprehensive study: Hubertus Lutterbach, *Gotteskindschaft. Kultur- und Sozialgeschichte eines christlichen Ideals*, Freiburg etc. 2003, pp. 165-256, esp. pp. 165-91.
5. Carola Reinsberg, *Ehe, Häterentum und Knabenliebe im antiken Griechenland*, Munich ²1993, p. 194. Harald Patzer, *Die griechische Knabenliebe*, Sitzungsberichte der Wissenschaftlichen Gesellschaft an der Johann Wolfgang Goethe-Universität Frankfurt am Main 19,1, Wiesbaden 1982, is fundamental to understanding the Greek love of boys and is also important for the history of research.
6. Reinsberg, *Ehe, Häterentum und Knabenliebe* (n. 5), pp. 164f.
7. John J. Winkler, *Der gefesselte Eros. Sexualität und Geschlechterverhältnis im antiken Griechenland*, Marburg 1994, p. 35.
8. Reinsberg, *Ehe, Häterentum und Knabenliebe* (n. 5), p. 163.
9. Ibid.
10. Ibid., p.170.
11. Elke Hartmann, 'Päderastie', in *Der Neue Pauly* 9, 2000, cols 139–41: 140. In col.139 she remarks: 'Scholars assess the status of the sexual and pedagogical aspects of pederasty [in antiquity] in different ways, sometimes interpreting it as a sexual relationship reined in by education and sometimes as education with an erotic colouring, in which the education of the citizen to be brave in war stands in the foreground.'
12. K. J. Dover, *Greek Homosexuality*, London 1978, with numerous illustrations in the central part of the monograph.
13. Reinsberg, *Ehe, Häterentum und Knabenliebe* (n. 5), p. 163.
14. Ibid., p.182.
15. Ibid., p. 188.
16. Ibid., pp.199–301.
17. Ibid., p. 86.
18. Werner Krenkel, 'Prostitution' in Michael Grant (ed), *Civilization of the Ancient Mediterranean. Greece and Rome* (2 vols), New York 1988, Vol. 2, pp. 1291–7.

19. Bettina Eva Stumpp, *Prostitution in der römischen Antike*, Antike in der Moderne, Berlin 1998, p. 205.

20. Ibid., p. 206.

21. Werner Krenkel, 'Pueri meritorii', *Wissenschaftliche Zeitschrift der Wilhelm-Pieck-Universität Rostock* 28,3, 1979, pp.179–89, esp. pp. 184f.

22. Stumpp, *Prostitution in der römischen Antike* (n. 19), p. 206.

23. Klaus Berger, *Theologiegeschichte des Urchristentums. Theologie des Neuen Testaments*, UTB für Wissenschaft. Große Reihe, Tübingen and Basel 1994, p. 42.

24. Peter Brown, *The Body and Society. Men, Women and Sexual Renunciation in Early Christianity*, New York and London 1988.

25. Ibid., p. 31.

26. Ibid.

27. Justin Martyr, *Apologia pro Christianis* 1, 27 ed Jean-Paul Migne, Patrologia Graeca 6, Paris 1857, cols 369B–372B; Basil the Great, *Homilia in Hexaemeron* VIII, 5 ed Jean-Paul Migne, Patrologia Graeca 29, Paris 1857, cols 177A–B (Greek), 178A-B (Latin).

28. Tertullian, *Apologeticum* 9 ed Heinrich Hoppe, Corpus Scriptorum Ecclesiasticorum Latinorum 69, Vienna and Leipzig 1939, pp. 23ff.

29. Stumpp, *Prostitution in der römischen Antike* (n. 19), p. 33.

30. For the development of the Stoic view of sexuality see Johannes Stelzenberger, *Die Beziehungen der frühchristlichen Sittenlehre zur Ethik der Stoa. Eine moraltheologische Untersuchung* (1933), Hildesheim etc. 1989, pp. 403–9.

31. Thus most recently after a discussion of the passages in question Holger Tiedemann, *Die Erfahrung des fleisches. Paulus und die Last der Lust*, Stuttgart 1998, p. 240; Marc D. Smith, 'Ancient Bisexuality and the Interpretation of Romans 1,26–27', *Journal of the American Academy of Religion* 64, 1996, pp. 223–56 agrees, taking special note of Rom.1.26; for the reception of the Pauline view in church history see Hubertus Lutterbach, 'Gleichgeschlechtliches sexuelles Verhalten – Ein Tabu zwischen Spätantike und Früher Neuzeit?', *Historische Zeitschrift* 267, 1998, pp. 281–311.

32. Thus most recently Tiedemann, *Die Erfahrung des fleisches* (n. 31), pp. 210–22.

33. Christian Gnilka, *Aetas spiritalis. Die Überwindung der natürlichen Altersstufen als Ideal frühchristlichen Lebens*, Theophaneia 24, Bonn 1972, p. 207.

34. Mayke de Jong, 'To the Limits of Kinship. Anti-Incest Legislation in the Early Medieval West (500–900)' in Jan Bremmer (ed), *From Sappho to De Sade. Moments in the History of Sexuality*, London and New York 1989, pp. 36–59: 36f.

35. Hubertus Lutterbach, *Sexualität im Mittelalter. Eine Kulturstudie anhand von Bußbüchern des 6. bis 12. Jahrhunderts*, Archiv für Kulturgeschichte. Beihefte 43, Cologne and Weimar 1999.

36. Heinz Wilhelm Schwarz, *Der Schutz des Kindes im Recht des frühen Mittelalters. Eine Untersuchung über Tötung, Mißbrauch, Körperverletzung,*

Freiheitsbeeinträchtigung, Gefährdung und Eigentumsverletzung anhand von Rechtsquellen des 5. bis 9. Jahrhunderts, Bonner historische Forschungen 56, Siegburg 1993, p. 100.

37. Ibid., p.105. Similarly ibid., p.127.
38. Maria Lahaye-Geusen, *Das Opfer der Kinder. Ein Beitrag zur Liturgie- und Sozialgeschichte des Mönchtums im Hohen Mittelalter*, Münsteraner theologische Abhandlungen 13, Altenberge 1991.
39. Thus H. Müller, 'Sittlichkeitsverbrechen' in *Handwörterbuch zur deutschen Rechtsgeschichte* 4, 1990, cols 1672–9: 1676.
40. Thus Philippe Ariès, *Centuries of Childhood. A History of Family Life*, New York 1962.
41. Müller, 'Sittlichkeitsverbrechen' (n. 39), col. 1676.
42. Rebekka Habermas, 'Parent-Child Relationships in the Nineteenth Century', *German History* 16, 1998, pp. 43–55.
43. Müller, 'Sittlichkeitsverbrechen' (n. 39), cols. 1676f.
44. Klaus Lüdicke (ed), *Kommentar zum Codex Iuris Canonici* (5 vols), Vol. 5, Münster 2001, Can. 1395 §2: 'If a cleric has otherwise committed an offence against the sixth commandment of the Decalogue with force or threats or publicly or with a minor below the age of sixteen, the cleric is to be punished with just penalties.'
45. From a legal historical perspective see e.g. the investigation relating to Switzerland by Werner Würgler, *Unzucht mit Kindern nach Art. 191 StGB* (typescript dissertation), Diessenhofen 1976.
46. 'UNKinderrechtskonvention, Art. 19, 1' in Britta Lauenstein (ed), *Die UN-Kinderrechtskonvention in Deutschland – verbindlich, aber unbekannt?*, Denken und Handeln 38, Bochum 1999, pp. 83–98: 93.
47. Reinhardt Jung, 'Die Kinderrechtskonvention der Vereinten Nationen. Übersetzt in die Sprache der Menschen, für die diese Konvention gedacht ist' in Britta Lauenstein (ed), *Die UN-Kinderrechtskonvention in Deutschland* (n. 46), pp. 99–107: 104.
48. For the noteworthy reflection that the measures provided for by church law against sexual interference with children by priests fall short of the normative standard of the UN Convention on the Rights of the Child see, in connection with Germany, the contribution to the discussion under http://www.ikvu.de

Operative Theologies of Priesthood: Have they Contributed to Child Sexual Abuse?

EAMONN CONWAY

Introduction

This article argues that in order to deal justly and responsibly with child sexual abuse by clergy, consideration must be given to operative theologies that may have colluded with and facilitated abusive behaviour.

Abusive behaviour is understood to be of two kinds. The first is the sexual abuse of minors by individual clergy. The second is the experience of abuse suffered by victims when they reported their abuse to church personnel. Victims have noted that the second kind of abuse, the suspicion, mistrust and even hostility that their reporting of the abuse elicited from church representatives, was sometimes more difficult to come to terms with than the initial criminal act of abuse.[1] Both forms of abuse prompt questions regarding deeply-held, taken-for-granted constructs, values, beliefs and identities operative in the Christian community.

Responsibility for the child sexual abuse crisis in the Catholic Church is generally considered by church leadership to lie entirely with a small number of individual priests whose crimes resulted from personal failure and sinfulness.[2] Similarly, church leadership tends to hold individual bishops responsible for the fact that cases of abuse were not dealt with adequately, rather than consider possible institutional failure.

Psychologists and psychotherapists, among them Marie Keenan (Ireland), Martin Kafka (USA), Bill Marshall and Karl Hanson (Canada), are convinced that there are particular developmental and situational factors, as well as factors relating to the socialization of clergy, at work in the clerical sexual abuse of minors. Their clinical research needs theological and structural consideration. In arguing for such consideration, there is no intention to seek to exonerate individual clergy abusers who remain ultimately responsible for their abusive behaviour.

This article will focus its consideration of operative theologies and their possible link to child sexual abuse on understandings of priesthood. However, other operative theologies also merit consideration, for example, images of God and the theologies of revelation that underpin them, as well as operative models of church and their influence upon the exercise of power. Reflection is also needed on the theology of sexuality operative especially in the formation of clergy.

I. Distinctive factors in clerical sexual abuse

We need to be cautious when drawing inferences from statistical data regarding the nature and extent of child sexual abuse. Much if not most sexual abuse remains unreported. Even when considering reported sexual abuse, much of the data relevant to our investigation has yet to be gathered and analysed properly. In general, however, it is accepted that the percentage of clergy who offend is less than the percentage of abusers in the general adult male population.[3] It follows that child sexual abuse is not mainly a church related problem. Nonetheless, a number of points need consideration here. The first relates to the distinctive profile of clergy offender.

For example, priest offenders frequently work out of a harsh and negative God imagery, evidence of a relationship with God based upon fear and guilt rather than upon unconditional love.[4] This in itself may not be distinctive of clergy offenders, but clergy offenders have had a distinctive theological formation programme, and the presence of this kind of God imagery raises serious questions about its nature and adequacy.

Also in need of consideration is the fact that at least 50% of clergy abusers have themselves been victims of sexual abuse, possibly more than is generally the case among offenders.[5] How many of these men found opportunities during their initial and on-going formation to deal with their experience of being abused?

Clergy offenders tend to have a higher IQ than most other sexual abusers, with a corresponding strong tendency to rationalize and intellectualize, but a diminished capacity to explore feelings and emotions.[6] Therapists also note a tendency among clergy abusers to view authority as lordship and power as control, and to have seriously unresolved psychological issues relating to conflict and authority. Sexual abuse is often as much about control and power as it is about sexuality. The control which sex offenders exercise over their victims can serve as a compensation for the powerlessness they feel in other aspects of their lives.[7] Aspects of church structure and organization that convey or exacerbate a sense of powerlessness among clergy therefore merit consideration in terms of situational factors that may contribute to the sexual abuse of minors.

According to Connors (1999), 90% of clergy offenders abused 'adolescents who did not threaten their own emotional development. In blunt psychodynamic terms, the abuser was more often than not an emotional adolescent preferring the company and affection of a chronological adolescent.'[8]

There is considerable clinical evidence that unlike sexual offenders generally in society, the vast majority of clergy who have abused minors have as their sexual preference post-pubertal boys.[9] This raises the issue of the relationship between sexual abuse of minors by clergy, and sexual orientation.[10] Psychotherapists are beginning to note that many, perhaps a majority, of the clergy who abuse minors have a homosexual orientation. It would be unfounded on the basis of this observation to suggest a direct causal link between a homosexual orientation and sexual abuse, since those with a heterosexual orientation also abuse minors. Abusers, whether homosexual or heterosexual in orientation, abuse because they have failed to develop mature, adult, peer-oriented integration of their sexuality. However, the observation that a majority of clergy offenders have a fundamentally homosexual sexual orientation gives pause for consideration. If it is clear that a homosexual orientation *per se* does not cause sexual abuse of minors, and equally clear that not all priests who are homosexual abuse, then we must ask if there is something in the life experience of a proportion of homosexual clergy that leads them to abuse. Situational factors seem the obvious place of enquiry, and such enquiry must also consider how these factors might differ from those impacting on clergy with a heterosexual orientation who abuse.

A basic question is whether or not the church's teaching and pastoral practice with regard to homosexuality actively serves to inhibit homosexuals, and perhaps particularly those who are priests, from growing into sexual maturity and from integrating their sexuality appropriately into their personal identity.[11] If there is also a disproportionately high number of clergy who are homosexual in orientation, then we also need to ask why this is the case, and evaluate the impact of this on the life and mission of the church.[12]

The reality is that for decades, sexuality was a taboo subject in both the initial and on-going formation of clergy. Sexual issues and urges were either 'spiritualized' or thrust underground, and a commitment to celibacy was embraced by many priests as an escape from exploring their capacity for intimacy, as release from having to come to terms in a mature way with sexuality. For many priests, the experience of ministry continues to be characterized by isolation. It is an experience of being burdened with unrealistic expectations, of being given many demanding roles with hardly any affirmative support or forms of accountability. What deeply-held, taken-for-granted theological presuppositions lie behind this particular structure and experience of ministry? We will go on to examine this in a moment. Before doing so, we must recall that victims have experienced two kinds of abuse, and so far we have alluded only to the actual sexual abuse. The abuse by the institution in its inability to handle matters also needs theological reflection.

II. Church response and management

Recent research into child sexual abuse by clergy in Ireland commissioned by the Irish episcopal conference concluded that:

> Responses to those abused by Church personnel were characterised by lack of outreach, communication, sensitivity and compassion. The overall impression was that Church personnel were more concerned with legal issues . . .[13]

This echoes a finding of the Office of the Attorney General of the Commonwealth of Massachusetts with regard to child sexual abuse in the Diocese of Boston. The report noted 'an institutional reluctance to address adequately the problem (of child sexual abuse) and, in fact, made choices that allowed the abuse to continue'.

But the Boston report is even more critical. It speaks of:

• The 'systemic abuse of children' that was enabled by the 'culture of acceptance of child sexual abuse within the Archdiocese'.
• 'The widespread sexual abuse of children due to an institutional acceptance of abuse and a massive failure of leadership.'[14]

The findings of these and other reports, if ignored, will damage the church's core mission in the service of the faith. Responsible engagement with these findings involves consideration of the culture of management and leadership operative in the church and the theologies that underpin it. It is not enough simply to change personnel (bishops), as has happened in a number of dioceses where the mishandling of abuse cases has been most publicized by the media.

We will now move to a consideration of theologies that may collude with or facilitate abusive behaviour in the church. The focus in this limited consideration will be upon professed and operative theologies of priesthood.

III. Two understandings of priestly office

We can identify two related but distinct understandings of the priestly office current in the church. On the one hand, there is emphasis on the priesthood as representative of Jesus Christ *to* the Christian community. In this, the prevalent understanding, the priest is understood in a unique way as *repraesentatio Christi* and the distinction between the priest and the Christian community is considered foundational to the church.

The contrasting model, which begins to re-emerge at the Second Vatican Council, refers to the priest as *repraesentatio ecclesiae*. Here, the emphasis is on the priest as representing the church understood as the Christian community under the guidance of the Holy Spirit. With this second model, the emphasis is on unity, on belonging, before distinction. The priest is one *of and with* the community before he stands over against it or ministers to it. His ministry flows from the apostolic nature of the church, the responsibility for which rests in the first instance with all the baptized.

In what follows I intend to outline some key aspects of both of these models. In the final section of this article I will explore their implications with regard to child sexual abuse by clergy and its handling by ecclesial authorities.

1. The priest as repraesentatio Christi

A high point in the development of the understanding of priesthood as *repraesentatio Christi* was the Council of Trent, where, against the Reformers, Trent stressed the essential difference between priests and the faithful. In this understanding, the priest is not a second mediator alongside Christ in the church. He *is* Christ at work, building up the church.[15] The priest in a unique way is understood as *alter Christus*. He acts *in persona Christi capitis,* and the emphasis is on the distinction rather than the unity between the head and the body of the church. Insistence upon obligatory celibacy and distinctive dress amplify the separateness and distinctiveness of the office. The priest is one who stands apart, his very life a sacrificial offering for the sake of the church.

In terms of priestly spirituality, this model of priesthood found expression in a prayer from Lacordaire that was frequently used by clergy. Priests were expected:

To live in the midst of the world with no desire for its pleasures.
To be a member of every family, yet belonging to none;
To share all sufferings, to penetrate all secrets, to heal all wounds;
To go daily from men to God to offer Him their homage and petitions:
. . . O Priest of Jesus Christ.'

James Joyce captured how the priest as *repraesentatio Christi* was perceived among the faithful:

To receive that call, Stephen . . . is the greatest honour that the Almighty God can bestow upon a man. No king or emperor on earth has the power of the priest of God . . . the power, the authority, to make the great God of Heaven come down upon the altar and take the form of bread and wine. What an awful power, Stephen![16]

The official catechism of the Council of Trent even spoke of priests as 'not only angels, but also gods, holding as they do amongst us the power of consecrating and offering the body of the Lord'.[17]

2. *The priest as* repraesentatio ecclesiae

Augustine wrote 'With you, I am a Christian; for you, I am Bishop.'[18] If the model of priest as *repraesentatio Christi* emphasizes 'for you', the model of priest as *repraesentatio ecclesiae* stresses 'with you'. The priest is first and foremost 'a man chosen from among men, a member of the church, a Christian' (Rahner).

According to this model, the faith of the church is witnessed to in a special way by the first apostles, but the church originates not in the apostles but in that to which they bear witness under the Spirit.[19] It is the Christian community rather than the priest alone that is *alter Christus*. The priest as *repraesentatio ecclesiae* gathers and presides over the faith of the church as people of God. He enables and facilitates the Christian community's proclamation of the gospel. Hence, the term presbyter is considered more appropriate than priest, which is used only of Israelite priests and of Christ in the New Testament.

By way of shorthand, we can say that the priest who sees himself as *repraesentatio Christi* will be at home with a more cultic understanding of his office, and with the language of priest-sacrifice-altar. The priest who understands himself as *repraesentatio ecclesiae* will understand his role more communally and prefer the language of presbyter-table-companionship.

In what way are these theologies operative in the life of the church?

IV. The findings of Priester 2000 ©[20]

A recent survey of almost 3,000 bishops, priests and seminarians in sixteen dioceses in five European countries conducted by Paul Zulehner at the University of Vienna three years ago provides some insights into the theological self-understanding of contemporary clergy.[21] Broadly speaking, four clergy 'types' emerge from the survey.

1. The 'man of Christ unaffected by the signs of the times' (*der zeitlose Kleriker*):

- understands his ministry as strictly and uniquely *repraesentatio Christi;*
- derives authority from Christ through the bishop, not through the community;
- is distanced from contemporary culture and undisturbed by 'the signs of the times' – the gospel is preached in season and out of season;
- considers ministry principally as sacramental;
- understands tradition statically, as the *depositum fidei* which he is to serve and protect;
- is concerned with unity between priests, bishops and the pope;
- except for retreats and spiritual direction, is unlikely to see the need for on-going formation;
- is uncomfortable with change and avoids risks;
- considers clerical dress, titles and symbols of office important.

Zulehner characterizes this type as the *anxious warden* or *sentinel*. According to the survey, this clergy type is most frequently found in leadership positions in the Catholic Church.

2. The 'man of God open to the signs of the times' (*der zeitoffene Gottesmann*):

- understands ministry both as *repraesentatio Christi* and *repraesentatio ecclesiae*;
- stresses his role as prophetic, and especially gives a voice to the voiceless in society;
- is concerned with unity among the hierarchy (vertically) but equally among the community (horizontally);
- after the celebration of the eucharist, considers preaching and giving spiritual advice the most important parts of his ministry;

- lives with the tension between church and world, the sacred and the pro-
fane, and seeks to serve as a bridge;
- is comfortable with shared decision-making;
- is more person- than task-oriented.

Priests of this type are found most frequently in middle management in the church. They are often elected by their brother priests to representative positions because they are *bridge-builders*: between church and world, *repraesentatio Christi – repraesentatio ecclesiae*, and so on.

3. The 'man of the church responsive to the signs of the times' (*der zeit-nahe Kirchenmann*):

- understands ministry first and foremost as *repraesentatio Christi*;
- sees his vocation as personal from Christ and therefore does not necessarily have or desire a close relationship with a parish community;
- sees his vocation as a profession, and carefully distinguishes between his private and public life;
- is very professional in his dealings with people; capable of fulfilling joyfully the different roles a priest finds himself in, from celebrant to school manager;
- values on-going education in, for example, media and communications, psychology and economics, but not necessarily theology;
- listens and consults but make his own decisions.

This category of priest is frequently found in academic circles as well as church leadership. Of all the types, he has least interest in or particular commitment to a local community and for him, unity as such, whether vertical or horizontal, is of less importance. Zulehner describes him as the *lonely wolf.*

4. Finally, 'the community leader in tune with the times' (*der zeitgemässe Gemeindeleiter*):

- is fundamentally committed to the common priesthood of all the faithful and is least at ease with the distinctions between lay and cleric;
- stresses the charismatic nature of the church, and facilitates joyfully the diversity of gifts in the community;
- finds nourishment for his spirituality in service rather than sacraments;
- is least likely to be concerned about directives from Rome;
- is uncomfortable with having to make or implement top-down decisions;
- values highly discussion and consensus decision-making.

Zulehner sees this fourth type as *the man on the margins*, the one least likely of the four types to be promoted within the church.

V. Models of priesthood among clergy who abuse minors

The final part of this article considers the implications of professed and operative models of priesthood for the child sexual abuse crisis in the Catholic Church. We examine if there are any conclusions we can make both with regard to the nature and extent of child sexual abuse by clergy and also with regard to the handling of child sexual abuse cases by those in authority.

As we have no information regarding the operative models of priesthood of offenders, we can say very little in this regard. We can only can speculate, which we now do briefly.

The *anxious warden* or *sentinel* is likely to be very disciplined and conscious of the sacredness of the priesthood and therefore the least likely to want to bring it into disrepute. His friendship circle is likely to consist more of other clergy than lay people, which might mean less contact with children at least in a family setting. On the other hand, he is the type most likely to exude a sense of the sacredness and power of the priesthood, something that victims have noted as characteristic of their abuse and as contributing to their sense of powerlessness.[22] This first type of priest is likely to have very rigid views on celibacy, which could be both a strength and a weakness. He is likely to rationalize rather than explore emotions, a point noted by therapists of clergy offenders, and is also least likely to want to seek therapy if in difficulty, instead relying on the grace of the sacrament of reconciliation to overcome his sinfulness and failings.

Priesthood understood as *repraesentatio Christi* could collude in a priest avoiding dealing with fundamental issues of human development and formation if emphasis in this model is placed on being a representative of the divinity of Christ. Effectively a denial of the incarnation, this would be detrimental not only to the humanity of Christ but to the priest's own humanity as well with possible tragic results.

The *bridge-builder* at least at first glance would seem to be more outgoing with a strong commitment to those on the margins of society, to the vulnerable and to the weak. This should mean sensitivity to powerlessness and therefore a keen desire to avoid exploitation of any kind. However, we know that sadly many of the victims of clergy come from the margins and are abused in the context of seeking help. The priest's orientation towards the community should mean less isolation in his ministry and openness to personal support if needed. On the other hand, being more outgoing and person-oriented may mean being in a better position to abuse trust.

The very term *lonely wolf* might alarm us in the context of child sexual abuse. But this need not necessarily be the case. This type shares with the *anxious sentinel* a sacral and therefore powerful sense of his office. But unlike the *sentinel*, the *wolf* separates his vocation from his personal life. This could be a danger signal, as he may see what he does in his private life as his own business. On the other hand, he is the least likely type of priest to be stressed and lose control. Like the *bridge-builder*, the *lonely wolf* is outgoing and is likely to be well-liked by the community, able to get and seek support if needed, at the same time likely to have ready access to children especially in a school context. However, his is the category that places most value on the expertise of others, e.g. psychologists.

Finally, the *man on the margins*, as the name suggests, is likely to be somewhat isolated and in need of support. He is also likely to lack a clear sense of role identity, and be in conflict with authority. This may cause him stress. He is likely both to be at ease with people and least critical of contemporary culture, including attitudes to sexuality. Being somewhat uncomfortable with priestly ministry, he is least likely to seek to overpower people with the sacral nature of his office. His strong sense of the individual giftedness of each of God's people should mean that he would seek to cherish people rather than violate them. At the same time, he is the most likely to experience a certain frustration and sense of powerlessness within church structures, and this could serve as a trigger for abusive behaviour.

Such speculations are of limited use. Theological models are not everything, and priests in all four categories are clearly at risk of sexually abusing if they have unresolved issues relating to psychosexual maturity. However, operative theologies of priesthood clearly influence the presence of certain risk factors such as isolation, proximity to community, attitudes to authority, the experience of power and powerlessness, resistance to human development and on-going formation etc.

One step towards protection of children and towards the renewal of priesthood would be to identify these risk factors further and put structures and processes in place to minimize them. Priests and seminarians in their formation stage should be encouraged to reflect on their own operative theology of priesthood and assess its strengths and weaknesses. The positive implications of such an exercise extend well beyond avoidance of possible misconduct to embrace the flourishing of a priest's ministry and the well-being of the Christian community as a whole.

VI. Models of priesthood and church management of child sexual abuse

We can speak with greater certainty about the influence of operative theological models of priesthood on the handling of child sexual abuse. Zulehner's survey confirms that the majority of those in decision-making positions in the church are working out of an understanding of priesthood as *repraesentatio Christi*. Those who understand priesthood primarily as such find it hardest to accept that priests could commit abusive acts.

This explains the initial sense of shock and outrage among those in church leadership at abuse revelations, and why there seemed in church circles to be as much concern about the damage done by clergy offenders to the institution of the priesthood as there was about the hurt and violation caused to victims. Add to this consideration of the sacredness of the vow of celibacy, and how for centuries it had been exalted above marriage. Shock often leads to denial, which was very much a feature of the early stages of the abuse crisis. It is also understandable that those in leadership working out of the *repraesentatio Christi* understanding of priesthood would have believed that clergy offenders could be helped simply by confession and spiritual direction.

The dominance of the *repraesentatio Christi* model also explains the priority given by church leaders to protecting the church and the priesthood. The *anxious guardian* or *sentinel* suffers when the reputation of the church and of the priesthood is tarnished on his watch. People who know bishops personally comment that these men for the most part are not preoccupied with a sense of their own power or self-importance, despite the image often portrayed in the media. It is true, however, that bishops share an overwhelming and lonely sense of responsibility for the church, the burden of which they see resting squarely on their shoulders.

When it comes to dealing with clergy abusers, those operating out of a very sacral notion of priesthood are likely to feel torn. On the one hand, they feel very let down by clergy abusers, and feel that those who have betrayed their office should be punished by dismissal. In some cases dismissal has been insisted upon without due regard to the duty of on-going care for offenders, indicating that it might be as much about punishment for betrayal as concern for the healing of victims or for child protection.[23] On the other hand, we have seen that some church leaders have been anxious to avoid allowing the teaching on the indelible character of ordination to be undermined by making dismissal from the clerical state too readily available as a sanction.[24]

The *repraesentatio Christi,* especially the kind who is at a distance from contemporary culture, is the least likely to seek and value the advice of or indeed trust those who do not have the grace of the sacrament of ordination. He is also least likely to accept that he should be accountable horizontally, for example to lay bodies in the church or to secular bodies in society. He is also least likely to see why he should be responsive to the media and be least moved by their repeated coverage of abuse cases.

The *bridge-builder* in leadership would be likely to seek to mediate between the authority of the magisterium, the authority of reason, e.g. theology and other sciences, and the authority of experience that resides in the community. The *anxious sentinel,* on the other hand, will rely solely on the authority of Rome and the advice of his fellow bishops. Criticism from other quarters is likely to leave him untouched. The *lonely wolf,* who, like the *sentinel,* works out of an understanding of *repraesentatio Christi,* is also likely to be happy with a clear line from the top, but will wish to make up his own mind independently if needs be. Valuing professionalism, he would also be least likely to have problems dismissing clergy offenders or dealing somewhat clinically with victims with the co-operation of lay experts such as lawyers and psychologists.

Conclusion

There is reason for concern that the model of the priest as *repraesentatio Christi* is not serving the church well. At the very least, it needs to be complemented by an understanding of priest as *repraesentatio ecclesiae.* This model would place greater value on a shared style of ecclesial leadership, with a balance between vertical as well as horizontal systems of accountability. Priesthood understood primarily as *repraesentatio ecclesiae* would provide the basis for a greater diversity of human experience in the church's official leadership. While there is no foundation to the claim that there is a direct link between celibacy and sexual abuse of minors, celibacy, embraced obligatorily simply as part of the priestly package, could well be an impediment to achieving sexual maturity.

In order to respond fully to the crisis of child sexual abuse, it would seem advisable:

- to develop the theology of priest as *repraesentatio ecclesiae,* building on the teaching of the Second Vatican Council;
- to promote this theology actively in programmes of initial and continuing formation for clergy;

- to encourage priests to reflect on their own operative theology of priest-hood, paying particular attention to their understanding of their own power and authority;
- to help priests to identify particular weaknesses and risk factors associated with their operative theology of priesthood and address these;
- to evaluate openly and honesty the church's professed and operative theology of sexuality.

The dominant images of priesthood assumed and promoted in the theological training and in the sub-cultures of seminaries have been put under a spotlight of suspicion in these pages. Some of their unquestioned assumptions may foster attitudes unworthy of the gospel and indeed capable unwittingly of facilitating sexual and other types of abuse. Both for the sake of its mission, and for the sake of those who have suffered and continue to suffer because of abuse by clergy, the church has a moral obligation to acknowledge and critically evaluate structural issues relating to child sexual abuse in the church and devise new structures of authority and accountability.

Notes

1. See H. Goode, H. McGee and C. O'Boyle, *Time to Listen. Confronting Child Sexual Abuse by Clergy in Ireland*, Dublin: Liffey Press 2003, pp. 141–42.
2. See John Paul II, *Address to Priests, Holy Thursday 2002*. A partial expression of corporate responsibility is found in the Pope's Apostolic Exhortation, *Ecclesia in Oceania* (2001). The dispute between the Vatican and the US Bishops' Conference, involving an initial rejection of the so-called 'zero-tolerance' policy proposed by the American bishops arguably is evidence that there are some voices within the Vatican that see the importance of considering contextual issues which contribute to clergy sexual abuse. See *http://www.nationalcatholicreporter.org/word/pfw1022.htm. Thursday, 24 October 2002 and http://nat-cath.org/NCR_Online/archives2/2002d/110102/110102d.htm. Friday, 28 March 2003.*
3. See T. Plante, 'A Perspective on Clergy Sexual Abuse', *San Jose Mercury News*, 24 March 2002, Opinion Section, and http://www.psywww.com/psyrelig/plante.html. Plante estimates the number of clergy offenders as between 2% and 5%. See also C. Bryant, 'Psychological Treatment of Priest Sex Offenders', *America*, April 2002, p. 14, who estimates the general population of paedophiles as 3% to 6%. A. R. Sipe, *Bless me Father for I have Sinned*, Connecticut: Praeger 1999, pp. 114–21, estimates the percentage of clergy abusers at 7% to 10%, higher than generally in society.
4. M. Keenan, 'Child Sexual Abuse: the Heart of the Matter', *The Furrow*, November 2002.

5. Plante states that 70% of clergy have themselves been abused. Bryant's research at St Luke's Institute (Washington) places the figure of clergy abusers who were themselves abused at 50%, still higher than their estimation of the general population of abusers at 30%.

6. C. Bryant, 'Psychological Treatment of Priest Sex Offenders', *America*, April 2002, p.17; T. Plante, 'Can Psychology help a Church in Crisis', *Monitor on Psychology* (Journal of the American Psychological Association), Vol. 33, June 2002.

7. See Olive Travers, *Behind the Silhouettes*, Belfast: Blackstaff 1999, p. 74; E. Conway, 'The Service of a Different Kingdom' in E. Conway, E. Duffy and A. Shields, *The Church and Child Sexual Abuse – towards a pastoral response*, Dublin: Columba Press 1999, pp. 76–90. See also H. Goode et al. (n. 1), pp. 186–88. Bishops and delegates interviewed for the RCSI report considered a power-orientated culture, characterized by centralization of power and authority, to be least dominant in existing church culture.

8. C. Connors, 'Psychological Perspectives on Priesthood'. Address to the National Federation of Priests' Councils, March 1999 (http://www.nfpc.org/COLLOQUIA/MARCH-1999/connors.html)

9. Data relating to offender profiles comes from two sources: treatment centres for offenders, and surveys of victims. Data from treatment centres for offenders in Ireland (M. Keenan, awaiting publication) accords with findings at Southdown (Canada) and St Luke's Institute (Washington) that identify clerical sexual abuse as predominantly that of post-pubertal boys. Goode et al. (n. 1), however, conclude on the basis of 39 victims of clerical sexual abuse recorded in the Sexual Abuse and Violence in Ireland (SAVI) report commissioned by the Dublin Rape Crisis Centre that 'most acts of clerical sexual abuse in Ireland are paedophile in nature and that only a small number of cases could be classed as ephebophile (abuse of male adolescents) or adult homosexual in nature'. Given that most sexual abuse of minors goes unreported, however, weight must be given to the data resulting from treatment centres for clergy.

10. Personal notes from conversation with Marie Keenan, January 2004.

11. See B. McMillan, 'Scapegoating in a time of crisis', *The Furrow*, May 2002; P. Jenkins, *Pedophiles and Priests – Anatomy of a Crisis*, OUP 1996, pp. 103–4; D. Cozzens, *The Changing Face of Priesthood*, Collegeville: Liturgical Press 2000, pp. 101ff; D. Cozzens, *Sacred Silence*, Collegeville: Liturgical Press 2002, ch. 8; J. Berry, *Lead us not into Temptation. Catholic Priests and the Sexual Abuse of Children*, Chicago: University of Illinois Press 2000, pp. 183–89; J. Gramick (ed), *Homosexuality in the Priesthood and the Religious Life*, NY: Continuum 1989; J. Alison, *Faith beyond Resentment*, London: Darton, Longman and Todd 2001, esp. p. 188.

12. See D. Cozzens, *The Changing Face of Priesthood* (n. 11), ch. 7.

13. H. Goode et al. (n. 1), p.141.

14. Office of the Attorney General – Commonwealth of Massachusetts, 'The

Sexual Abuse of Children in the Roman Catholic Archdiocese of Boston –
Executive Summary and Scope of Investigation', 23 July 2003.

15. For an outline of the two models see P. Hünermann, 'Mit dem Volk Gottes
unterwegs. Eine geistliche Besinnung zur Theologie und Praxis des kirchlichen
Amtes' in *Geist und Leben* 54 (1981), pp.178–87. See also R. Gaillerdetz,
'Shifting Meanings in the Lay-Clergy Distinction', *Irish Theological Quarterly*,
Vol 64/2 (1999), pp. 115-40.

16. James Joyce, *A Portrait of the Artist as a Young Man,* London: Grafton Books
1916.

17. *Catechism of the Council of Trent*, Part 3 ch.7, Q.11.

18. Augustine, Sermo 340, 1.

19. See P. Hünermann (n. 15). See also B. Nolan, 'What difference does Priestly
Ordination make?' in J. H. Murphy (ed), *New Beginnings in Ministry*, Dublin:
Columba Press 1992, pp. 128–59.

20. See P. Zulehner and. A. Hennersperger, '*Sie gehen und werden nicht matt' (Jes
40,31), Priester in heutiger Kultur*, Ostfildern: Schwabenverlag 2001.

21. The countries concerned were: Germany, Croatia, Austria, Switzerland and
Poland. As only European countries are represented, one must be cautious
about drawing inferences for other continents e.g. India and Latin America.

22. See E. Conway, 'The Service of a Different Kingdom' (n. 7).

23. See E. Conway, 'Care for Clergy Offenders', *The Furrow*, May 2003, pp.
218–24; J. Beal, 'It shall not be so among you!' in F. Oakley and B. Russett,
Governance, Accountability and the Future of the Catholic Church, New York:
Continuum 2003, p. 89.

24. See, for example, the Vatican critique of the original version of the US Catholic
Conference of Bishops' Dallas Charter (June 2002). A comparison of the original and revised versions is available at http://www.boston.com/globe/spot
light/abuse/extras/policy_comparison.htm

III. Consequences for Governance, Canon Law and Pastoral Theology

'As Idle as a Painted Ship upon a Painted Ocean': A People Adrift in The Ecclesiological Doldrums

JOHN P. BEAL

I. The sex abuse crisis as a crisis of ecclesial leadership

The sexual abuse crisis, which has engulfed the Catholic Church in the United States, especially since early 2002, has become an ecclesial leadership crisis. Although public attention has focussed on the unfolding of this crisis in North America, especially the United States, the pattern of sexual abuse of minors by priests and irresponsible handling of complaints of abuse by bishops has been a worldwide phenomenon.[1] Moreover, the scope and duration of the events that have given rise to this crisis suggest that it cannot be dismissed as a media event involving only a few particularly perverse priests and a few especially inept bishops. Seemingly endless media reports of clergy abuse and its mishandling by bishops has sparked public outcry for greater transparency, accountability, and participation in ecclesial governance. Nevertheless, 'quick fixes', like tightening the disciplinary norms for clergy, enacting diocesan and national policies for responding to complaints and fostering a 'safe environment' in the church, and establishing review boards to monitor compliance with these norms and policies,[2] while important and even necessary in their own right, may be insufficient to address the deeper problems that allowed the clergy sexual abuse problem to fester quietly until it erupted as a full-blown crisis.

What lies at the heart of the crisis is a more pervasive malaise that has prompted one knowledgeable observer to describe the American church, even without the sex abuse crisis to serve as a dramatic reference point, as 'a people adrift'.[3] Often overshadowed by the coverage of the sexual abuse crisis itself are other, less newsworthy symptoms of a people adrift: the not always successful struggle to define and maintain the Catholic identity of charitable and educational institutions,[4] the abject failure to hand on even a rudimentary knowledge of the Catholic tradition to the next generation,[5] the painful mediocrity of most parish liturgies even after forty years of liturgical renewal,[6] and declining levels of participation in and sense of adherence to the Catholic Church.[7] What the sexual abuse crisis added to this picture of the church as 'idle as a painted ship upon a painted ocean' has been the wrenching sense that even 'the very deep did rot'.

II. The ecclesiological climate in which the crisis festered

Long before the sexual abuse crisis in the Catholic Church erupted on the public scene in early 2002, there were conditions in the body ecclesiastic that created a climate in the church which did not cause, but did foster the conditions for the episcopal mismanagement which transformed the tragic and too frequent incidents of sexual abuse into a full-blown crisis.

1. A truncated 'communion' ecclesiology

Prior to the Second Vatican Council, the official ecclesiology of the Catholic Church emphasized the visible and juridic features which the church as a *societas perfecta* had in common with the other 'perfect society,' the state. Vatican II attempted to redress the relative neglect of the invisible and spiritual elements of the church in the ecclesiology of a *societas perfecta* by retrieving the patristic ecclesiology of communion. However, as it was incorporated into the conciliar documents and eventually the revised Code of Canon Law, this communion ecclesiology assumed a form that has been described as 'christomonistic', in that it gives a rather one-sided emphasis to the role of Christ in constituting and empowering the church through word and sacrament and seriously neglects the mission of the Holy Spirit in the church.[8]

This communion ecclesiology is reasonably successful in drawing attention to the church as a community of baptized believers, all of whom share a common life in Christ and are endowed with their own spiritual gifts to contribute to the edification of the church, and as a communion of local, episcopally governed churches in communion with one another and with the

Bishop of Rome. However, this ecclesiology so accentuates the role of Christ, the invisible Head of the church, made sacramentally visible through those configured to him in a unique way through sacred ordination that there is little role left for the Holy Spirit in the church, except to preserve in the truth already received.[9] In virtue of their configuration to Christ, the ordained are empowered to serve *in persona Christi Capitis* as heads of the local churches in the case of bishops and as head of their communion in the case of the Bishop of Rome. As a result, the ordained teach, sanctify and govern the people of God or the portion of it entrusted to their care with sacred power. In this respect, they 'represent' Christ the Head by making him visibly present in the community of the faithful.[10]

This christomonism of the conciliar communion ecclesiology has resulted in a pronounced tendency to identify the teaching, sanctifying and governing activities of the ordained with Christ himself and to situate the ordained over-against the community of faithful rather than within it.[11] The problem with this ecclesiology is not that it is essentially hierarchical or that it attributes a central role to the ordained, especially the Bishop of Rome and the diocesan bishops in communion with him. It is hard to imagine an authentically Catholic ecclesiology that did not do so. Rather, the problem is that, in this ecclesiology, all power in the church, all authentic teaching, sanctifying and governing, are conceived as proceeding in one direction, downward from Christ through the ordained to the faithful. Little provision is made for the counterflow one would expect to find in a genuinely trinitarian ecclesiology, upward from the Spirit-filled community of the faithful with its rich endowment of charisms to the church's hierarchical officers and ultimately to the triune God. Instead, the only roles 'in the church' this ecclesiology leaves for the non-ordained (and those at the lower end of the hierarchy) are passive-assenting to authoritative teaching, receiving sacramental ministrations, and obeying legitimate directives.[12] The charisms of the non-ordained are conceived as much more oriented to their vocation to work 'in the world' in the manner of leaven.

In this communion ecclesiology, all lines of accountability lead upward from the faithful, to presbyters and deacons, to the bishop, to the pope, and ultimately to Christ, rarely horizontally to fellow bishops, presbyters, deacons and ministerial collaborators and never downward to those entrusted to the pastoral care of the ordained. Thus, church leaders imbued with this communion ecclesiology are also prone to resist the suggestion that they need to learn before they teach, be sanctified before they sanctify, and listen before they govern. Since they teach, sanctify and govern in the name and in the person of Christ, they are prone to extend the mantle of their charism of office to all their teaching, sanctifying and governing activity and to view expressions of disagreement or dissent, even on mundane administrative matters, as signs of disloyalty not only to the office holder personally but ultimately to Christ.

Since this communion ecclesiology was intended to serve as a counterweight to the one dominant 'perfect society' ecclesiology with its explicit acceptance of the analogy between the church and the state, its protagonists reject the use of political and social science categories for understanding the church as secularizing trends and threats to the integrity of the church's *sui iuris* nature as a purely theological reality.[13] Such ecclesiological monophysitism often lies behind rejections of demands for accountability of church leaders to the faithful with the mantra, 'The church is not a democracy.' At a superficial level, this curt dismissal simply states the obvious; at a deeper level, however, it represents a radical rejection of the relevance of the human sciences for probing the mystery of the church. Thus, for a church leader to assert baldly that the church is not a democracy is somewhat akin to a business executive arrogantly proclaiming that he does not need to bother himself with market research. Consequently, the one-directional flow of the communion ecclesiology underlying the conciliar documents and the revised code can foster the climate in which the ordained 'are in danger of living in [the midst of the faithful], separated from them by a haze of fiction'.[14] Bishops operating in a 'haze of fiction' have been all too much in evidence during the current crisis.

2. Bureaucracy trumps structured participation

The tendency of the one-way flow of teaching, sanctifying and governing power sanctioned by the communion ecclesiology of the conciliar documents and the revised code to insulate hierarchical authorities from countercurrents arising from below is reinforced by the existence of large bureaucracies which assist bishops and the Bishop of Rome in the governance, respectively, of their particular churches and the universal Church. The Roman Curia has a long history of being a major player in the governance of the universal Church.[15] Diocesan curias mushroomed first in the aftermath of the Modernist crisis of the early twentieth century and then again in the wake of Vatican II to assist bishops in the ever more complex tasks of diocesan pastoral governance.[16] The emergence of these bureaucracies was both inevitable and necessary to provide efficient pastoral service for ever larger and more diverse churches. The personal, hands-on style of governance characteristic of bishops in the patristic era simply would not work for the pope of a world church or a bishop of a teeming urban diocese with millions of souls or even a sprawling rural diocese encompassing tens of thousands of square miles.

Nevertheless, bureaucracies of their nature tend to insulate the hierarchical leaders they serve from direct involvement with the joys and hopes, griefs and anxieties of the faithful and to establish themselves as permanent centres of influence and power. Bureaucracies monitor the upward flow of information along the hierarchical chain of command and tend to filter out information that is discouraging, disturbing or dissenting from the agendas of the hierarchical leaders – and of the bureaucracy itself. In turn, bureaucracies are conduits for the downward flow of information from leaders to lower units of the organization and ultimately to the subjects of the organization's ministrations. Since knowledge and expertise are the source of power in an organization, bureaucracies tend to dole out only as much information as those lower on the chain of command need to carry out their assigned functions. Through careful management of the upward and downward flow of knowledge and expertise, bureaucracies generate a condition of permanent dependency in their clients. Thus, bureaucracies become effective agents of command and control from above but poor agents for empowerment of, or even listening to, those at the 'grass roots'.[17]

These bureaucracies at the heart of the universal church and the particular churches have reinforced the one-directional momentum of the prevailing christomonistic communion ecclesiology and have effectively marginalized consultative structures, both new and old, which were intended to give a voice in church governance to the governed and to give expression to the essentially synodal dimension of the church.[18] At the level of the universal church, the Synod of Bishops, which was intended to provide a regular forum for dialogue between the pope and bishops throughout the world, has been hijacked by the Roman Curia.[19] Although the regular synods are held, their 'deliberations' now result in papal exhortations that could have been written – and sometimes seem to have been written – even without the bishops' contribution.[20] At the level of the particular church, recent Vatican norms seem to have been designed to impose the same stringent limits on free discussion at diocesan synods that have become the norm for the Synod of Bishops.[21] Moreover, almost nowhere has the presbyteral council (or the now moribund cathedral chapter) emerged as a genuine voice 'to aid the bishop in the governance of the diocese' (c. 495, §1), and finance and pastoral councils at both the diocesan and parish levels have been largely ineffective in providing a voice of the faithful in diocesan and parish governance.[22] As a result, official structures for facilitating the exercise of the faithful's right 'to make known their needs' and 'their opinion on matters to pertain to the good of the church' both to church leaders and to other members of the faithful (c. 212, §§2–3), where they exist, have proved too weak and deferential to be effective vehicles for communication between the faithful and church leadership, especially when they have given voice to painful truths or nagging dissatisfactions leaders would prefer not to hear. The unavailability of effective institutional vehicles for the faithful to make known their needs and opinions on matters pertaining to the good of the church in a timely manner has contributed to the metastasizing of the sexual abuse scandal into an ecclesial crisis.

3. Identification of the good of the church with the good of the institution

When the official ecclesiology enshrined in conciliar documents and the Code of Canon Law and reinforced by the inherent dynamics of centralized bureaucracies leave church leaders operating 'in the haze of fiction', it is difficult for these leaders to avoid the temptation to identify the good of the church with the good of the institution they represent (a good which often corresponds closely to their own interests as a class). That church leaders succumbed to this temptation before and during the current crisis can hardly be doubted. Overwhelming evidence shows that bishops almost everywhere attempted to protect the public image of the church by denying, ignoring or minimizing complaint, by exhibiting more concern for the reputation and rehabilitation of troubled priest abusers than for the needs of their victims or the prevention of further abuse, and by withholding information about sexual abuse by priests and particular priest abusers from the faithful in general and from those who would minister with or be ministered to by these clerics in subsequent assignments.[23] One cannot escape the impression that church leaders were so consumed by the need to maintain the appearance of health and holiness in the church that they were paralysed when confronted by the cancer of evil eating away at the heart of the church.

One would like to think that, having been chastened by the experience of the last few years, church leaders have learned to recognize that the real good of the church as a community of the faithful is not always identical with the perceived good of the church as an institution and that neglecting the former inevitably also damages the latter at least in the long run. Evidence that church leaders have learned this painful lesson is not, however, reassuring. If in the past church leaders sought to serve the good of the institution by suppressing or minimizing evidence of sinfulness in the church, now they seem intent on purging the church or at least the ranks of its clergy of any perception of sinfulness. As Richard John Neuhaus has acerbically observed:

> The niceties of canon law, due process, and elementary decency have in many instances taken a beating. As one cardinal archbishop said after Dallas, it may be necessary for some priests to suffer injustice for the good of the Church. In the course of history, Caiaphas has not been without his defenders. . . . Another reaction claims to be realistic, which is to say hard-nosed: it's too bad that some innocent priests may be hurt, but you can't make an omelet without breaking eggs, etc. Charming. But then, bishops have their own leadership credibility to worry about.[24]

Responding to evidence of the sinfulness of and in the body ecclesiastic by denial, minimalization and rationalization and by radical amputation of every member even suspect of infection are both tactics which betray a failure to distinguish the good of the church from the good of the institution, a failure common to mandarin classes who operate 'in the haze of fiction'.

4. Penalizing exit, suppressing voice

In his study of decline in firms, organizations and states, Albert Hirschman identifies two options available to those dissatisfied with the decline in quality of the organization's performance or product to make their dissatisfaction known to the organization's leadership: exit and voice.[25] The dissatisfied exercise the option of 'exit' when they stop buying the product and turn to a similar product supplied by a competitor or withdraw from the organization totally or partially; they exercise the option of 'voice' when they make their dissatisfaction known directly to the leadership of the organization. In the business world, where brand loyalty tends to be relatively weak, customers manifest their dissatisfaction with the decline in quality of a company's product by shifting to a competitor's comparable brand (the 'exit' option). Evidence of declining sales then alerts the management of the need to redress the decline in quality of its product or suffer further loss of sales and, ultimately, extinction. In social organizations like the church where loyalty to the organization tends to be high, members usually voice their dissatisfaction more or less directly to the organization's leadership in the expectation that remedial action will be taken (the 'voice' option) and will resort to the 'exit' option only after they reach total frustration at the leadership's unresponsiveness.[26]

The resiliency of an organization, its ability to survive and even overcome

inevitable declines in the quality of its performance, depends on the effectiveness of exit, voice or some combination of the two in capturing the attention of the organization's leadership and prompting remedial action to arrest
or reverse declining performance. The leadership of the Catholic Church
has long been conspicuously unresponsive to expressions of dissatisfaction
from below by exit, voice, and various combinations of the two. The relative
equanimity with which church leaders accepted the widespread departure of
priests from the active ministry during the 1970s and since has prompted
observers to classify the church as a 'lazy monopoly'.[27] The unresponsiveness to 'voice' characteristic of a 'lazy monopoly' has also been exhibited by
church leadership in their relative indifference to criticism from below of the
flaccidity, mediocrity, and deterioration in quality of various aspects of
church life, most recently in the bishops' handling of widespread dissatisfaction with the way they had dealt with the sexual abuse crisis.

The Catholic Church has been quite successful in fostering a high degree
of organizational loyalty among the faithful. To the extent that they have
appropriated and internalized the church's claim to be the society in which
the one, holy, catholic, and apostolic church of Christ subsists, the faithful
pay a high price for exercising the 'exit' option in response to dissatisfaction
with inadequate or deteriorating organizational performance. However,
church leaders have actively discouraged the faithful from exercising the
'voice' option (e.g., by silencing dissident theologians, refusing to engage in
serious discussion and sometimes even to meet with groups or individuals
critical of current policy and practices, and denying use of church facilities
for meetings of groups which have not been fully co-opted and placed under
the control of church authorities) and turned deaf ears to those who do exercise 'voice', until, as in the current crisis, the outcry becomes too thunderous
to ignore. The christomonistic communion ecclesiology of the conciliar
documents and the revised code provides the ideological superstructure,
and centralized bureaucracies at both the universal and local levels of the
church provide the practical infrastructure for delegitimizing, marginal-
izing, and sometimes demonizing of the 'voice' of the faithful and blunting
its effectiveness as a catalyst for remedial action to arrest decline in and
improve mediocrity of the church's performance as a religious organization.

III. Conclusion

Hirschman's conclusion about the fate of organizations that make no explicit
allowance for either 'exit' or 'voice' from arresting institutional decline are
ominous for the Church if it continues its present drift:

Exit is here considered as treason and voice as mutiny. Such organizations are likely to be less viable, in the long run, than the others; exit and voice being illegal and severely penalized, they will be engaged in only when deterioration has reached so advanced a stage that recovery is no longer either possible or desirable.[28]

Since the Catholic Church cannot consistently claim that the church of Christ subsists in it and encourage those dissatisfied with declining quality of church performance to exercise their 'exit' option, it must find ways to make the 'voice' option available and effective for the faithful. To insist on the necessity of effective 'voice' for the church to arrest its decline into a people adrift is not, however, to insist that the church become a democracy. Organizations as irredeemably hierarchic and undemocratic as large multi-national corporations and the military have found ways to alert leaders to decline in quality and performance and to prompt them to remedial action. Nevertheless, making the 'voice' option available and effective will require a more balanced and trinitarian ecclesiology than the one-directional, christomonistic communion ecclesiology that now prevails in magisterial documents and canon law and an overhaul of the bureaucratic infrastructure designed more for command and control from above than for facilitation of initiative and communication from below. Faith tells us that it will be the breath of the Holy Spirit that ultimately provides the breeze to prevent the church from remaining permanently adrift in its current doldrums. It would be presumptuous, however, for those at the helm to refuse to unfurl the sails to catch that breeze when, in God's good time, it comes. It was, after all, human folly that once led to a crew of poor souls being cast adrift 'as idle as a painted ship upon a painted ocean'.

Notes

1. For a discussion of the unfolding of the crisis in Ireland, Great Britain and other parts of Europe, see G. Mannion, '"A Haze of Fiction": Legitimation, Accountability, and Truthfulness' in F. Oakey and B. Russett (eds), *Governance, Accountability, and the Future of the Catholic Church*, New York 2003, pp. 161–17.

2. See United States Conference of Catholic Bishops, 'Charter for the Protection of Young People, Revised' and 'Essential Norms for Diocesan/Eparchial Policies Dealing with Allegations of Sexual Abuse of Minors by Priests or Deacons, Revised', *Origins* 32, No. 25, 28 November 2002, pp. 411–18: 409.

3. For the imagery and much of the substance of what follows, I am indebted to P. Steinfels, *A People Adrift: The Crisis of the Roman Catholic Church in America*, New York 2003.

4. Ibid., pp. 103–61.
5. Ibid., pp. 203–41 and, in greater depth, D. R. Hoge, W. D. Dinges, M. Johnson and J. Gonzalez, *Young Adult Catholics*, Notre Dame 2003.
6. See Steinfels (n. 3), pp. 165–202.
7. See W. Dinges, D. Hoge, M. Johnson and J. Gonzalez, 'A Faith Loosely Held: The Institutional Allegiance of Young Catholics', *Commonweal*, 17 July 1998, pp. 13–18.
8. E. J. Kilmartin, 'Lay Participation in the Apostolate of the Hierarchy', *The Jurist* 41 (1981), pp. 352–62.
9. Ibid., p. 361.
10. Ibid., pp. 352–57.
11. Ibid., p. 361.
12. See A. Dulles, 'Changing Concepts of Church Membership' in *The Resilient Church*, New York 1977, pp. 135-38.
13. See the repeated invocation of this slogan in D. Wuerl, 'Reflections on Governance in the Church' in Oakley and Russett, *Governance, Accountability, and the Future of the Catholic Church* (n. 1), pp. 13–24. The view is articulated in a more theoretical framework in E. Corecco, 'Synodal or Democratic Structure of the Particular Church' and 'Ecclesiological Bases of the Code' in G. Borgonovo and A. Cattaneo (eds), *Canon Law and Communio*, Vatican City 1999, pp. 70–102 and 284–96 and in J. Ratzinger, 'Freedom and Constraint in the Church' in *Church, Ecumenism and Politics*, New York 1988, pp. 182–203.
14. Yves Congar, *Power and Poverty in the Church*, London 1964, as cited in G. Mannion, 'A Haze of Fiction' (n. 1), p. 161.
15. See A. M. Stickler, 'Le riforme della Curia nella storia della Chiesa' in P. A. Bonnet and C. Gullo (eds), *La Curia Romana nella Cost. Ap. 'Pastor Bonus,'* Vatican City 1990, pp. 1–16 and T. J. Reese, *Inside the Vatican*, Cambridge 1996, pp. 106–39.
16. See J. H. Provost, 'Diocesan Administration: Reflections on Recent Developments' *The Jurist* 41 (1981), pp. 81–104; K. M. McDonough, 'Beyond Bureaucracy: New Strategies for Diocesan Leadership', *CLSA Proceedings* 61 (1999), pp. 251–66; and id., 'Diocesan Bureaucracy,' *America* 177, 11 October 1997, pp. 9–13.
17. On the operation and tendencies of bureaucracies in general, see M. Weber, *The Theory of Social and Economic Organization*, New York 1964, pp. 329–40. For their operation in the particular church, see J. Provost, 'Toward a Renewed Canonical Understanding of Official Ministry', *The Jurist* 41 (1981), pp. 463–469 and K. McDonough, 'Diocesan Bureaucracy'(n. 16), pp. 11–12.
18. See P. Granfield, 'Legitimation and Bureaucratization of Ecclesial Power', *Concilium* 197 (1988), pp. 86–93. On the synodal element of the church, see W. Aymans, *Das synodale Element in der Kirchenverfassung*, Munich 1970 and the various studies collected in *Das konsoziative Element in der Kirche*, St Otilien 1989 and *La Synodalité. La participation au gouvernement dans l'Église*, Paris 1992.

19. T. Reese (n. 15), *Inside the Vatican*, pp. 55-65.
20. See J. Grootaers and J. Selling, *The 1980 Synod of Bishops 'On the Role of the Family': An Exposition of the Events and an Analysis of its Text*, Leuven 1983, on the lack of influence of the Synod and its deliberation on the resulting apostolic exhortation *Familiaris consortio*.
21. See Congregation for Bishops and Congregation for the Evangelization of Peoples, *Instructio de Synodis diocesanis agendis*, 19 March 1997: *AAS* 79 (1997), pp. 706–27.
22. See J. Provost, 'The Working Together of Consultative Bodies – Great Expectations?' *The Jurist* 40 (1980), pp. 257–81.
23. See The Investigative Staff of *The Boston Globe*, *Betrayal: The Crisis in the Catholic Church*, Boston 2002 for an overview of the situation in the United States. For an equally distressing overview of the situation in Great Britain, see Nolan Review, *Review on Child Protection in the Catholic Church in England and Wales*, www.nolanreview.org.uk/.
24. R. J. Neuhaus, 'In the Aftermath of Scandal,' *first Things*, February 2004, p. 60.
25. A. O. Hirschman, *Exit, Voice and Loyalty: Responses to Decline in firms, Organizations, and States*, Cambridge 1970, pp. 3–5.
26. Ibid., pp. 76–105.
27. J. Seidler, 'Priest Resignations in a Lazy Monopoly', *American Sociological Review* 44 (1979), p. 774. The characteristics of a 'lazy monopoly' are: '(1) The organization is a virtual monopoly – i.e., has singular control over a resource or product. (2) Executives are slow to improve the quality of product, policies, or the structure of the organization. (3) Executives, rather than improving quality, prefer to lose clients or personnel who exercise voice (criticism). (4) They welcome opportunities for critics to exit, often via limited competition. (5) These opportunities allow the continuation of status quo policies or mediocre leadership, as a loss of critics reduces the pressure for change and usually leaves the remnant on the conservative or uninvolved side.' See Hirschman (n. 25), pp. 57–75.
28. Hirschman (n. 25), p. 121.

Sexual Abuse as an Offence in Canon Law

A plea for a consistent application of the existing legal norms of the Catholic Church

HANS–JÜRGEN GUTH

Both state law and church law prohibit sexual abuse.[1] Although the details of what is defined as sexual abuse differ in the various legal systems, both state and church legal systems assume that sexual abuse always occurs when another person is forced to perform an undesired action which has sexual connotations without that person's agreement. State prosecutors and church authorities can as a rule take action only when they have been made aware of such illicit actions either through an informant or in another way. The obligation actively to take preventative measures against unwanted sexual harassment and interference which goes beyond the penal sanctions that apply in individual cases has appeared only recently in state law and in church law.

However, when it comes to penal sanctions for sexual abuse, church law can refer back to a long tradition. Unfortunately this tradition also shows that there has always been sexual abuse in the church. For had there been no cases, then they would not have been incorporated in early church penitential books and collections of law.[2] The collection called *Corpus Iuris Canonici* developed at the level of the universal church into the most significant work; at the latest after the edition by the *Correctores Romanes* it even had quasi-official character.[3] Church law arose as a collection of legal decisions in specific cases to which reference was then made to form the basis of decisions in similar cases. This 'case law', which is still predominant in Anglo-Saxon jurisprudence, was largely replaced in continental European law by legislation in the form of law books promulgated by the legislators. For the Catholic Church this came about through the *Codex Iuris Canonici* of 1917 (CIC 1917),[4] which in 1983 was replaced by a new *Codex Iuris Canonici* (CIC 1983).[5] Since 1990 there has likewise been a law book for the Eastern churches united with Rome, the *Codex Canonum Ecclesiarum Orientalium* (CCEO).[6]

As James Provost has demonstrated, in the *Codex Iuris Canonici* of 1917, for the first time in an official legal text of the Catholic Church sexual

misdemeanours were described as an offence against the sixth commandment of the Decalogue.[7] The decisions collected in the *Corpus Iuris Canonici*
mention individual offences in very concrete terms, as they are based on a
particular situation. Occasionally other descriptions of the situation can be
found. The key definition of the 1983 *Codex Iuris Canonici* which applies
today has taken over the description of sexual transgressions as an offence
against the sixth commandment in its canon 1395 from canon 2359 of CIC
1917. By contrast the parallel prescription in CCEEO speaks in canon 1453
of a sin against the commandment of chastity and contains no explicit reference to the sixth commandment of the Decalogue. The same goes for the
special case of sexual abuse in connection with the confessional which is
specifically regulated in canon1387 CIC 1983 or canon 1458 CCEO. Both
universal law books of the Catholic Church which are currently valid contain
only these provisions in connection with sexual abuse or sexual transgressions which relate exclusively to clergy and religious. In the pre-Codex law,

canon 1395 CIC 1983	canon 1453 CCEO
1. A cleric who lives in concubinage, other than the case mentioned in canon 1394, and a cleric who persists with scandal in another external sin against the sixth commandment of the Decalogue is to be punished by a suspension. If he persists in the delict after a warning, other penalties can gradually be added, including dismissal from the clerical state. 2. A cleric who in another way has committed an offence against the sixth commandment of the Decalogue, if the delict was committed by force or threats or publicly or with a minor below the age of sixteen years, is to be punished with just penalties, not excluding dismissal from the clerical state if the case so warrants.	1. A cleric who lives in concubinage or otherwise persists in an external sin against chastity causing scandal is to be punished with a suspension. If he persist in the delict, other penalties can gradually be added, including deposition. 2. A cleric who has attempted a forbidden marriage is to be deposed. 3. A religious who has taken a public, perpetual vow of chastity and is not in sacred orders, is to be punished with an appropriate penalty if he or she has committed these delicts.

as still in CIC 1917 (Cann. 2357 and 2357), there are also provisons which apply to all the baptized.

canon 1387 CIC 1983	canon 1458 CCEO
A priest who in the act, on the occasion, or under the pretext of confession solicits a penitent to sin against the sixth commandment of the Decalogue is to be punished, according to the gravity of the delict, by suspension, prohibitions, and privations; in graver cases he is to be dismissed from the clerical state.	A priest who in the act, on the occasion, or under the pretext of confession, has solicited a penitent to sin against chastity, is to be punished with an appropriate penalty, not excluding deposition.

With the *motu proprio Sacramentorum sanctitatis tutela* of 30 April 2001[8] and the letter of the Congregation of the Doctrine of the Faith of 18 May 2001[9] published at the same time the jurisdiction over delicts against morality committed by a cleric on a person who has not yet reached the age of eighteen were transferred to the Congregation of the Doctrine of Faith. According to canon 1405 §1 nos 2 and 3 CIC 1983, jurisdiction over offences committed by bishops and cardinals lies exclusively with the pope. For the sphere of the Latin Church in all other cases it is the responsibility of the diocesan bishop in question to institute appropriate proceedings.[10] This also follows clearly from canon 277 §3 CIC 1983. The parallel stipulation in canon 374 CCEO instead refers quite generally to particular law. Canon 277 CIC 1983 and canon 373 or canon 374 CCEO form so to speak the basis for the regulations given above.

The regulations in the two church law books cannot be presented in detail here (Cann.1717–1731 CIC 1983 and Cann.1468–1487 CCEO).[11] But both books contain detailed regulations for a form of legal proceedings, even if this is only very rarely implemented.[12] There are several reasons for this. One may be the restraint towards legal proceedings which is formulated in both codices.[13]

Often not only a general lack of trust in viable resolutions of conflicts legitimated by church law but also a widespread ignorance of the relative regulations in church law even among bishops may be and is responsible for a mode of proceedings by church authorities in cases of sexual abuse which take place outside the existing law and are usually labelled 'pastoral'.[14] This means that the problem is fatally ignored and made taboo, with the result that the scandal of sexual abuse is even more offensive.[15] The tendency first

canon 277 CIC 1983	canon 373 CCEO
1. Clerics are obliged to observe perfect and perpetual continence for the sake of the kingdom of heaven and therefore are bound to celibacy, which is a special gift of God by which sacred ministers can adhere more easily to Christ with an undivided heart and are able to dedicate themselves more freely to the service of God and humanity. 2. Clerics are to behave with due prudence towards persons whose company can endanger their obligation to observe continence or give rise to scandal among the faithful. 3. The diocesan bishop is competent to establish more specific norms concerning this matter and to pass judgment in particular cases concerning the observance of this obligation.	Clerical celibacy chosen for the sake of the kingdom of heaven and highly suited to the priesthood is to be greatly esteemed everywhere, according to the tradition of the entire Church; likewise, the state of married clerics, sanctioned in the practice of primitive Church and in the Eastern churches through the ages, is to be held in honour.
	canon 374 CCEO
	Clerics, celibate as well as married, should shine forth with the splendour of chastity; it is for particular law to establish suitable means to attain this end.

and foremost to seek the avoidance of scandal and to sweep it under the carpet can prove disastrous here. Only public proceedings can lead to speedy clarification, in particular in order to protect further potential victims, but also to disarm unjust charges and accusations. Those who think that they have to spare those concerned or the public by keeping things secret out of a false understanding of love of neighbour make themselves the accomplices of the perpetrator. This makes the scandal even greater, rather than limiting the damage, which is the hope.[16]

A further reason must also lie in canon 1344 no. 2 CIC 1983 or canon 1409 §1 no. 2 CCEO, which allows the judge not to impose a penalty if the guilty person 'has been or, it is foreseen, will be punished sufficiently by civil authority'. Yet another reason must be the extremely brief period of limitation provided for in church penal law; in general this amounts to three years;[17] according to canon 1362 1 no. 2 CIC 1983 or canon 1152 §2 no. 2 CCEO for a delict described in canon 1395 CIC 1983 or canon 1453 CCEO five years; and for the offences reserved for the Congregation of the Doctrine of Faith according to canon 1362 §1 no. 1 CIC 1983 or canon 1152 §2 no.1 CCEO in connection with the letter of the Congregation of the Doctrine of Faith dated 18 May 2001 and mentioned above ten years.

However, it is worth mentioning in this context that at the request or urging of the United States Episcopal Conference, the legislator for the whole church has modified the regulations applying to the universal church in the case of the USA. In particular, in addition to an extension of the periods of limitation, the age of minors in canon 1395 §2 CIC is raised to eighteen. The derogation of the otherwise universally valid norms of CIC 1983 which was issued by rescript applied in the USA from 25 April 1994, initially for a period of five years, which in the meantime has been extended by a further ten years to 25 April 2009.[18]

The guidelines published by the United States Episcopal Conference in 1995 are entitled 'Canonical Delicts involving Sexual Misconduct and Dismissal from the Clerical State'; this explains the relevant regulations in church law in a way which those who are not canon lawyers can also understand.[19] Subsequently individual dioceses in the USA have issued their own guidelines for dealing with the problem of sexual abuse in the service of the church or have modified guidelines which already exist.[20] So as not to increase the harm done by the far from inadequate way in which the problem of sexual abuse has been dealt with, the US Episcopal Conference not only approved a *Charter for the Protection of Children and Young People* on 14 June 2002,[21] but was also given the necessary recognition for the *Essential Norms for Diocesan/Eparchial Policies Dealing with Allegations of Sexual Abuse of Minors by Priest or Deacon*' in a rescript of the Congregation of Bishops dated 8 December 2002. Thus with their promulgation by the US Episcopal Conference, since 12 December 2002 these norms apply as particular law for the USA.[22] The Foreword to the guidelines runs: 'These norms are complementary to the universal law of the Church which has traditionally considered the sexual abuse of minors a grave delict and punishes the offender with penalties, not excluding dismissal from the clerical state if the case so warrants.' On the one hand these norms now commit all the dioceses in the USA to issuing their own guidelines for dealing with the problem of sexual abuse.[23] On the other hand the main concern of the norms is the consistent application of church law; this is addressed both by a large number of references to the relevant regulations and also directly.[24] Here the *Guide to the Implementation of the US Bishops' Essential Norms for Diocesan/Eparchial Policies Dealing with Allegations of Sexual Abuse of Minors by Priests or Deacons* published in 2003 by the Canon Law Society of

America is extremely helpful.[25] North American canon lawyers have concerned themselves time and again with this topic from the perspective of church law since 1986. A series of articles in the professional journal *The Jurist*, published in Washington DC,[26] and *Studia Canonica*, published in Ottawa,[27] is evidence of this.

In the German language Myriam Wijlens in 1996 was the first to deal extensively with aspects of sexual abuse in church law.[28] Otherwise it is only recently that German-language literature on canon law has dealt with this problem in connection with the guidelines 'On Dealing with the Sexual Abuse of Minors by clergy within the jurisdiction of the German Episcopal Conference', promulgated on 26 September 2002.[29] Unlike the US Episcopal Conference, the German Episcopal Conference has passed only voluntary legal guidelines. Even if these guidelines are meant to 'guarantee a uniform mode of procedure', their concrete implementation shows some differences in four dioceses chosen at random. They seem to me to be implemented most consistently in the archdiocese of Bamberg. Here there is an independent official representing the archbishop, i.e. an official whose work and terms of service so far have had no connection with the archdiocese, to examine charges of sexual abuse; he is supported by a staff of six.[30] The same thing also applies in the diocese of Limburg, where Dr Josefine Heyer, a pastoral psychologist and Mary Ward sister, has been appointed as the official responsible for dealing with sexual abuse; she is supported by a permanent staff under the chairmanship of the diocesan judge Dr Georg Bier.[31] The diocese of Rottenburg-Stuttgart has appointed a commission rather than an official to deal with sexual abuse.[32] The diocese of Trier has nominated just one official to deal with matters of sexual abuse.[33] There must be major objections to the fact that in the dioceses of Limburg and Rottenburg-Stuttgart, for example, heads of the personnel divisions are automatically members of the staff or the commission on sexual abuse. For if in questions of sexual abuse the staff or commission advise the diocesan bishop in accordance with diocesan regulations and are to provide support in supervising the organs of the episcopal administration, here in fact they are advising or controlling themselves. The nomination of the head of the personnel department as the official responsible for dealing with sexual abuse, as has happened e.g. in the diocese of Trier, also seems to me to be an illegitimate mixture of tasks which should be seen to be separate, regardless of the undoubted integrity of the person concerned.

Unlike modern constitutional legal systems, which are based on the principle of the division of authority into the legislative, executive and judicial arms, because of the unity of authority the church's legal system has only a functional division. However, what ultimately gets in the way of legal proceedings in the church is certainly not the notion of 'unity of authority'. Rather, we encounter the fear that e.g. in legal proceedings the diocesan bishop can no longer be the one who determines the procedure. As a rule, in cases of sexual abuse in principle canon 1720 CIC 1983 or canon 1486 CCEO, which are about what happens if the ordinary decides to proceed by a decree without a trial, cannot be cited here, because it does not allow adequate reaction either in terms of legal proceedings or in respect of the admissibility of the penalties to be imposed by decree. However, the potential solutions which are offered by the church system of justice for the problem of sexual abuse in the service of the church, which so far has been concerned almost exclusively with proceedings for annulling marriages, seem to me by no means to have been exhausted. The call for stricter norms[34] could thus prove superfluous if existing laws were applied consistently. Still, justified criticism of existing norms should be taken seriously by the relevant church legislators.

In the end, an open and transparent way of dealing with the problem of sexual abuse is the only possible way of resolving the scandal, and with it the even greater scandal that sometimes for decades the church authorities responsible either have been unwilling to take note of the problem or have even tried actively to cover it up. Now the church authorities, and especially the episcopal conferences, have taken a great variety of initiatives, not only in church law but in measures aimed at building up trust; this has happened not only in the USA and Germany but in many other countries, e.g. Canada, Ireland, England and Wales, Scotland, Austria and Switzerland.[35] The *motu proprio* of the legislator for the whole church, *Sacramentorum sanctitatis tutela* of 30 April 2001,[36] can also be included here. However, it would be desirable if the *Normae substantiales* and *Normae processuales* mentioned in the *motu proprio* were also published officially. Unfortunately, like the earlier *Instructio Crimen sollicitationes* of 16 March 1962, they were sent only to the local ordinaries. In addition to providing greater legal certainty this would doubtless not only have the preventative effect which the legislator for the whole church intends, but would also be a further measure in building up trust.

In his letter 'To Priests' of Holy Thursday 2002, Pope John Paul II addressed directly the problem of sexual abuse in the service of the church:

> At this time too, as priests we are personally and profoundly afflicted by the sins of some of our brothers who have betrayed the grace of ordination in succumbing even to the most grievous forms of the *mysterium iniquitatis*

at work in the world. Grave scandal is caused, with the result that a dark shadow of suspicion is cast over all the other fine priests who perform their ministry with honesty and integrity and often with heroic self-sacrifice. As the church shows her concern for the victims and strives to respond in truth and justice to each of these painful situations, all of us – conscious of human weakness, but trusting in the healing power of divine grace – are called to embrace the *mysterium Crucis* and to commit ourselves more fully to the search for holiness.[37]

An open, transparent and consistent application of existing regulations in the Catholic Church could regain lost trust, to the benefit not only of potential future victims of sexual abuse but also of all church workers and all Catholics. This would also allow the church as a whole to fulfil its task of once again proclaiming the gospel of Jesus Christ in society with complete credibility.

Translated by John Bowden

Notes

1. In this article the terms canon law and church law will be used as synonyms for the law of the Catholic Church. Of course there is also church law outside the Catholic Church. Thus for example the law of the Anglican Church as well as the law of the Catholic Church is termed canon law.

2. James H. Provost, 'Offenses against the Sixth Commandment: Toward a Canonical Analysis of Canon 1395', *The Jurist* 55, 1995, pp.632–63, esp. pp. 634–38; James A. Brundage, *Law, Sex, and Christian Society in Medieval Europe*, Chicago 1987.

3. Emil Friedberg (ed), *Corpus Iuris Canonici*, Vols 1–2, Leipzig 1879–1881, reprinted Graz 1959.

4. AAS 9, 1917, Part II. The edition quoted is *Codex Iuris Canonici. Pii Pontificis Maximi iussi digestus Benedicti Papae XV auctoritate promulgatus. Praefatione, fontium annotatione et indice analytico-alphabetico ab Petro Card. Gasparri auctus*, Rome 1974.

5. AAS 75 (1983) Part II. Quotations are from the bilingual edition: Canon Law Society of America (ed), *Code of Canon Law, Latin-English Edition, New English Translation*, Washington DC 1999.

6. AAS 82, 1990, pp.1033–364. Quotations are from the bilingual edition: *Code of Canons of the Eastern Churches*, Latin-English Edition, New English Translation, Washington, DC 2001.

7. Provost, 'Offenses against the Sixth Commandment' (n. 2).

8. AAS 93, 2001, pp.737–39. The text is on the home page of the Holy See:

http://www.vatican.va/holy_father/john_paul_ii/motu_proprio/docu-
ments/hf_jp-ii_motu-proprio_20020110_ sacramentorum-sanctitatis-tutela
lt.html.

9. AAS 93, 2001, pp.785-88. The text is on the home page of the Holy See:
http://www.vatican.va/roman_curia/congregations/cfaith/documents/rc_c
on_cfaith_doc_20010518_epistula_graviora%20delicta_lt.html.

10. Cf. canon 1060 §1 nos 1 and 2 CCEO. There are further exceptions in Eastern
church law as e.g. in canon 1063 § 4 CCEO.

11. See e.g. Wilhelm Rees, *Die Strafgewalt der Kirche. Das geltende kirchliche
Strafrecht – dargestellt auf der Grundlage seiner Entwicklungsgeschichte*, Berlin
1993; William H. Woestman, *Ecclesiastical Sanctions and the Penal Process. A
Commentary on the Code of Canon Law*, Ottawa 2000.

12. 'Even if the penal process hardly ever occurs in practice in church courts . . .',
thus e.g. Hans Paarhammer, 'Das Strafverfahren', in Joseph Listl and Heribert
Schmitz (eds), *Handbuch des katholischen Kirchenrechts*, Regensburg ²1999,
pp. 1212–22: 1212. The *Caput Tribunalia Dioecesium ac Regionum* in the
Annuarium Statisticum Ecclesiae issued annually by the Secretaria Status
Rationarum Generale Ecclesiae contains only tables and information about proceedings over marriages. This is certainly also to be seen as an indication of the
small number of other proceedings, especially legal penal proceedings. See e.g.
Secretaria Status Rationarum Generale Ecclesiae (ed.), *Annuarium Statisticum
Ecclesiae. Statistical Yearbook of the Church. Annuaire Statistique de L'Eglise
2001*, Vatican City 2003, pp. 411–89.

13. Canon 1341 CIC 1983 and canon 1718 CIC 1983 or canon 1403 CCEO, see also
canon 1446 CIC 1983 or canon 1103 CCEO.

14. 'When bishops decide to proceed extracanonically . . . ', John P. Beal, 'Have
Code, Will Travel: Advocacy in the Church of the 1990s', *The Jurist* 53, 1993,
pp. 319–43.

15. With reference to canon 1395 CIC 1983 as early as 1987 John G. Proctor
remarks: 'It is clear from the context of the canon itself that deliberate ignorance
of the offense or studied avoidance of the offender does little to remedy the
problem.' So for Proctor it is clear that: 'There can be no doubt that simple
transfer or removal of an offender is no longer an adequate response to these
situations, either in terms of civil law, nor in terms of ecclesial concern.' John
G. Proctor, 'Clerical Misconduct: Canonical and Practical Consequences' in
Canon Law Society of America (ed), *Proceedings of the Forty-Ninth Annual
Convention, Nashville, Tennessee, October 12–15, 1987*, Washington, DC 1988,
pp. 227–44: p. 231 n. 9 and p. 239.

16. Hans-Jürgen Guth, 'Nur kein Skandal: Thomas von Aquin und die
Vermeidung öffentlichen Ärgernisses im kanonischen Recht' in Winfried
Aymans, Stephan Haering and Heribert Schmitz (eds), *Iudicare inter fideles.
Festschrift für Karl-Theodor Geringer zum 65. Geburtstag*, Sankt Ottilien 2002,
pp. 121–27.

17. Canon 1362 §1 CIC 1983 or canon 1152 §2 CCEO.

18. See e.g. Thomas J. Green, 'Book VI. Sanctions in the Church. Canon 1395' in John P. Beal, James A. Coriden, Thomas J. Green (eds), *New Commentary of the Code of Canon Law. Commissioned by The Canon Law Society of America*, Mahwah, NJ 2000, pp. 1598–1601: pp.1600–01 n. 296, and John A. Alesandro, 'Dismissal from the Clerical State in Cases of Sexual Misconduct: Recent Derogations', *CLSA Proceedings* 56, 1994, pp. 28–67.

19. National Conference of Catholic Bishops (eds), *Canonical Delicts Involving Sexual Misconduct and Dismissal from the Clerical State*, Washington, DC 1995.

20. E.g. the Archdioceses of Los Angeles, California and Saint Paul-Minneapolis, Minnesota and the Dioceses of Lafayette, Indiana and Las Vegas, Nevada.

21. Home page of the United States Conference of Catholic Bishops: http://www.usccb.org/ocyp/charter.htm. See also now United States Conference of Catholic Bishops (ed), *Report on the Implementation of the Charter for the Protection of Children and Young People*, Washington, DC 2004. The report is also on the home page of the United States Conference of Catholic Bishops: http://www.usccb.org/ocyp/audit2003/report.htm.

22. Home page of the United States Conference of Catholic Bishops: http://www.usccb.org/bishops/norms.htm or home page of the Holy See: http://www.vatican.va/roman_curia/congregations/cbishops/documents/r c_con_cbishops_doc_20021216_recognitio-usa_en.html.

23. Norm 2, clause 1: 'Each diocese/eparchy will have a written policy on the sexual abuse of minors by priests and deacons, as well as by other church personnel.'

24. E.g. norm 2, clause 2: 'This policy is to comply fully with, and is to specify in more detail, the steps to be taken in implementing the requirements of canon law, particularly CIC, canons 1717–1719, and CCEO, canons 1468–1470', or norm 8 A, clause 1: 'A. In every case involving canonical penalties, the processes provided for in canon law must be observed, and the various provisions of canon law must be considered (cf. *Canonical Delicts Involving Sexual Misconduct and Dismissal from the Clerical State*, 1995; *Letter from the Congregation for the Doctrine of the Faith*, May 18, 2001).'

25. Canon Law Society of America (ed), *Guide to the Implementation of the US Bishops' Essential Norms for Diocesan/Eparchial Policies Dealing with Allegations of Sexual Abuse of Minors by Priests or Deacons*, Washington, DC 2003.

26. Bertram F. Griffin, 'The Reassignment of a Cleric Who Has Been Professionally Evaluated and Treated for Sexual Misconduct with Minors: Canonical Considerations', *The Jurist* 51, 1991, pp. 326–39; Peter Cimbolic, 'The Identification and Treatment of Sexual Disorders and the Priesthood', *The Jurist* 52, 1992, pp. 598–614; James H. Provost, 'Some Canonical Considerations Relative to Clerical Sexual Misconduct', *The Jurist* 52, 1992, pp. 615–41; John P. Beal, 'Doing what one can: Canon Law and Clerical Sexual Misconduct', *The Jurist* 52, 1992, pp. 642–83; John B. Hesch, 'The Right of the Accused Person to an Advocate in a Penal Trial', *The Jurist* 52, 1991, pp. 723–24; Francis G. Morrisey, 'Some Thoughts on Advocacy in Non-

Matrimonial Cases', *The Jurist* 53, 1993, pp. 301–8; John P. Beal, 'Have Code, Will Travel: Advocacy in the Church of the 1990s', *The Jurist* 53, 1993, pp. 319–43; John S. Grabowski, 'Clerical Sexual Misconduct and Early Traditions Regarding the Sixth Commandment', *The Jurist* 55, 1995, pp. 527–91; John Tuohey, 'The Correct Interpretation of Canon 1395: The Use of the Sixth Commandment in the Moral Tradition from Trent to the Present Day', *The Jurist* 55, 1995, pp. 592–631; James H. Provost, 'Offenses against the Sixth Commandment: Toward a Canonical Analysis of Canon 1395', *The Jurist* 55, 1995, pp. 632–63.

27. Michael Hughes, 'The Presumption of Imputability in Canon 1321 §3', *Studia Canonica* 21, 1987, pp. 19–36; Jerome E. Paulson, 'The Clinical and Canonical Considerations in Cases of Pedophilia: The Bishop's Role', *Studia Canonica* 22, 1988, pp. 77–124; Kenneth E. Fischer, 'Respondeat superior redux: May a Diocesan Bishop be Vicariously Liable for Intentional Torts of his Priests?', *Studia Canonica* 23, 1989, pp.119–48; Thomas P. Doyle, 'The Canonical Rights of Priests Accused of Sexual Abuse', *Studia Canonica* 24, 1990, pp. 335–82; Francis G. Morrisey, 'Procedures to be Applied in Cases of Alleged Sexual Misconduct by a Priest', *Studia Canonica* 26, 1992, pp. 39–73; John P. Beal, 'Administrative Leave: Canon 1722 Revisited', *Studia Canonica* 27, 1993, pp. 293–320; Kevin M. McDonough, '"I never knew what you really thought of me". Evaluation of Pastors and the Issue of Unassignability', *Studia Canonica* 32, 1998, pp. 145-56; Gregory D. Ingels, 'Protecting the Right to Privacy when Examining Issues Affecting the Life and Ministry of Clerics and Religious', *Studia Canonica* 34, 2000, pp. 439–66; Francis G. Morrisey, 'Addressing the Issue of Clergy Abuse', *Studia Canonica* 35, 2001, pp. 403–20.

28. Myriam Wijlens, 'Kirchenrechtliche Aspekte' in Stephen J. Rossetti and Wunibald Müller (eds), *Sexueller Missbrauch Minderjähriger in der Kirche. Psychologische, seelsorgliche und institutionelle Aspekte*, Mainz 1996, pp. 156–72.

29. The guidelines are to be found on the home page of the German Episcopal Conference, http://dbk.de, under the heading 'Schriften'. They have also been printed e.g. in *Amtsblatt des Bistums Trier*, 1 December 2002, pp. 244–6, and *Kirchliches Amtsblatt für die Diözese Rottenburg*-Stuttgart, 10 October 2002, pp. 181–4. The Festschrift for Richard Puza on his sixtieth birthday, Andreas Weiss and Stefan Ihli (eds), flexibilitas Iuris Canonici, Frankfurt am Main 2003 contains three relevant articles in German: Klaus Lüdicke, 'Der Glaubens-kongregation vorbehalten – Zu den neuen strafrechtlichen Reservationen des Apostolischen Stuhls' (pp. 441–55); Luc De fleurquin, 'Pädophilie und "episkopein". Maßnahmen der Bischofskonferenzen von England und Wales sowie von Irland und Schottland' (pp. 457–76); Rik Torfs, 'Die Entlassung aus dem Klerikerstand' (pp. 476–97). At the conference organized by Ludger Müller, Sabine Demel, Libero Gerosa, Alfred E. Hierold and Peter Krämer which was held from 7 to 9. March 2004 at the University of Bamberg on 'Penal Law in a Church of Love. Necessity or Contradiction?', a working party under

leadership of Alfred E. Hierold studied the topic 'Paedophilia: Church Protection for Victims and Accused'.

30. Home page of the archdiocese of Bamberg: http://www.eo-bamberg. de/eob/opencms/show_nachricht.html?f_newsitem_id=2827&f_action =show and http://www.eobamberg.de/eob/opencms/show_nachricht. html?f_newsitem_id=2826&f_action=show.

31. *Amtsblatt des Bistums Limburg*, 1 April 2003, pp. 147–8 and home page of the diocese of Limburg: http://www.bistumlimburg.de/index.php?page=000-009–001-000&eid=8353&type=theme.

32. *Kirchliches Amtsblatt für die Diözese Rottenburg-Stuttgart*, 10 October 2002, pp. 185-88 and home page of the diocese of Rottenburg-Stuttgart: http://www.drs.de/_Module/News_Anzeige.asp?NewsID=48& BereichID=7.

33. *Kirchliches Amtsblatt des Bistums Trier*, 1 December 2002, p. 247 and home page of the diocese of Trier: http://www.bistumtrier.de/cgi/editorsoffice?_SID= fake&_modus=suche&_bereich=artikel&_aktion= detail&idartikel=114604. See also http://www.wochenzeitung.paulinus.de/archiv/0249/bistuma3. htm.

34. 'In fact today large numbers of the world's bishops are expressing the wish for a tightening of penal law for example in the case of priests who have been found guilty of paedophilia.' Joseph Cardinal Ratzinger, 'Stellungnahme', *Stimmen der Zeit* 124, 1999, pp. 169–71: 170.

35. See e.g. the study commissioned by the Irish Episcopal Conference and published in 2003: Helen Goode, Ciarán O'Boyle and Hannah McGee, *Time to Listen: Confronting Child Sexual Abuse by Catholic Clergy in Ireland*, Dublin 2003.

36. AAS 93, 2001, pp. 737–9 (see n. 8).

37. *L'Osservatore Romano*, weekly edition in German, 29 March 2002, pp. 9–11: 11. Also on the home page of the Holy See: http://www.vatican.va/holy_father/ john_paul_ii/letters/2002/ documents/hf_jp-ii_let_20020321_priests-holy-thursday_ge.html

Child Abuse by Priests:
The Interaction of State Law and Canon Law

RIK TORFS

Introduction

During the past years, child abuse by priests initiated a very serious crisis in the Roman Catholic Church. The causes underlying this phenomenon have been analysed by various other authors in this *Concilium* issue. My personal angle is a legal one, which means concretely legal in a general, and not merely in a canonical way.

In the child abuse issue, canon law on its own, as an isolated discipline, was unable to offer satisfactory answers to the problem. It badly needed indirect help by state law, as well as by public opinion.

In my contribution, I shall first analyse the canonical norms and tools as formulated by the 1983 Code of Canon Law, and why they failed to deal successfully with child abuse by priests.

In a second section, the role of state law, including its increasing pressure on church structures will be at stake.

Finally, in a third section, some remarks with regard to the future role of both canon law and church-state relationships will be formulated.

I. The failure of canon law

At first glance, there is no reason why canon law should be structurally unable to cover successfully child abuse by priests. As a matter of fact, the Roman Catholic Church is very strict when it comes to sexual relationships in general. More specifically, priests are bound to observe perfect and perpetual continence for the sake of the kingdom of heaven, and therefore are obliged to observe celibacy (canon 277 §1 CIC 1983). Moreover, this general principle is concretised by several norms in book VI of the Code on sanctions in the church. Both the violation of celibacy (canon 1394) and various violations of clerical chastity (canon 1395) lead to severe sanctions. Child abuse is even explicitly mentioned in canon 1395 §2: 'If a cleric has

... committed an offence against the sixth commandment of the Decalogue with force or threats or publicly or with a minor below the age of sixteen, the cleric is to be punished with just penalties, including dismissal from the clerical state if the case warrants it.'

Given the clarity of these norms, everything looks fine. There is no good reason for scepticism concerning the church and its approach of child abuse by clerics. But then again, the facts prove that the church as an institution has been unable, in various countries, to deal with the issue of child abuse in a satisfactory way.

How can this failure be explained? Leaving aside psychological or theological reasons, the legal basis for the failure can be found in the 'explosive' combination of two factors, namely (a) the fact that the church still operates as a *societas perfecta* and (b) the observation that the legal culture within the church falls short of modern juridical standards. It is precisely the *interaction* of both elements that explains the disastrous results we are currently confronted with, as I shall try to explain.

1. The church as a societas perfecta

The Austrian canonist Franz Rautenstrauch (d. 1785) was probably the first author to make use of the notion *societas perfecta*.[1] He wrote: 'The Christian society is of divine origin. It is a perfect society.'[2] In the following century, many canonists developed the idea of *societas perfecta* more in depth, among them Taparelli (d. 1862), Tarquini (d. 1874)[3] and Cavagnis (d. 1906).[4] An excellent definition was offered by Joseph Kleutgen, who drafted the schema *Tametsi Deus* for the first Vatican Council. For him, *societas perfecta* is 'a society, distinct from every other assembly of men, which moves towards its proper end and by its own ways and reasons, which is absolute, complete, and sufficient in itself to attain those things which pertain to it and which is neither subject to, joined as a part, or mixed and confused with any society.'[5]

Clearly, *autonomy* is the key notion. The canonists used the term *societas perfecta* to refute the Protestant jurists who held that the church is not a perfect society but a *collegium* within the state. Furthermore, they defended the idea that both the church and the state, each in its own order, are perfect societies.

Pius XII[6] was the last pope to employ the notion of *societas perfecta* on occasion. Before Vatican II updated theological thinking, it was clear that the position of the *societas perfecta* developed as a theoretical construction to demonstrate the independence of the church from unjustified civil interference. But eventually, the idea of *societas perfecta* went beyond that scope and was used to describe the essence of the church: political and legal concepts entered theology.

Vatican II changed this situation. It no longer used the term *societas perfecta* in order to describe the church. Other descriptions emerged. The church was seen as a sacrament, people of God, body of Christ, and as a prophetic, priestly and eschatological society.[7]

It is true, however, that at the same time the notion *societas perfecta* was never openly rejected, not even at a theoretical level. While rejecting the *societas perfecta* on a theoretical level is (psychologically) difficult but possible, rejecting it on a more practical, legal level is even more hazardous, as the content of the Code of Canon Law (CIC 1983) adequately illustrates. The Code had the ambition to translate the ideas set forward by the Council, and yet, it often rather repeats and strengthens pre-conciliar thoughts. Especially with regard to the *societas perfecta*, it became clear that abandoning this notion on a legal level was not a realistic project. Canon 22 of the CIC 1983, part of book I on *General Norms*, offers a clear illustration of this idea: 'Civil laws to which the law of the church defers should be observed in canon law with the same effects, insofar as they are not contrary to divine law and unless it is provided otherwise in canon law.'

Ladislas Örsy, commenting on this canon in 1985, wrote: 'Most of the time canon law and civil law operate side by side, independently of each other; thus, there are many cases in which the same person, physical or juridical, is the subject of two distinct sets of rights and duties, one in canon law, another in civil law. If conflict arises, experts must find the best solution they can.'[8]

By writing the way he does, Örsy virtually admits the practical existence of the church as a perfect society. Obviously, this is what canon 22 really says. Canon law can defer freely to secular norms, although not always. In case divine law is involved, secular norms have to give way. God comes first. Moreover, even if divine law is not in danger, canon law remains autonomous. Church authorities can freely decide whether or not they want to make use of civil norms.

Clearly, the guiding principle is that the choice is with the church. A choice for and a choice against the applicability of secular norms are both possible; they are the mere result of a free decision taken by church authorities. Such a way of reasoning confirms a mindset inspired by the *societas perfecta* theory. The starting point of the approach is the complete freedom and autonomy of the church. The possibility of state law imposing certain norms on the church, for instance binding norms with regard to labour law or due process, is not even envisaged by canon 22. The relationship between canonical and secular norms is a one-way relationship: the church can include secular norms in its own system, but is never obliged to do so. It is quite clear that such a one-way choice could turn out to be slightly naïve in a modern democratic society. The latter tends to impose several minimum norms on all its citizens, including associations and religious groups. Quite often, these norms are connected with democracy and the rule of law. The fact that the church does not seem to be aware of this 'danger' (or trend, if one prefers a more neutral notion) shows how obvious and self-evident an implicit *societas perfecta* thinking remains in a canonical context.

2. *The poverty of canonical legal culture*

The canonical survival of the *societas perfecta* idea goes hand in hand with another phenomenon, namely the poverty of canonical legal culture. Although the Code, theoretically speaking, possesses an adequate set of norms, enough at least to tackle sexual abuse problems (canon 277, canons 1394 and 1395), the practical application of these norms remains problematic.

First, dismissal from the clerical state as a possible penalty for child abusers,[9] can rightly be imposed only by a judicial process (canon 1342 §2). The 'easier way' of an extra-judicial decree is not available. In practice, however, church tribunals lack expertise with regard to such judicial procedures. Most tribunals never dealt with them during their entire existence. Thus, a serious problem emerges: if (a) the church continues functioning as if it were a *societas perfecta* and (b) the proper internal procedures are, for technical and practical reasons, almost never applied, then true justice will not be done.

Secondly, the non-application of penal law is often ideologically motivated. Certainly, technical problems make the implementation of penal norms through a judicial process very difficult. Yet, not applying penal norms is also part of a solid church tradition. In that regard, canon 1341 is clear. A procedure for imposing penalties can be started by the ordinary 'only after he has ascertained that scandal cannot sufficiently be repaired, that justice cannot sufficiently be restored by fraternal correction, rebuke and other ways of pastoral care'. In other words, the more 'pastoral' approach so characteristic for the church entails that penal sanctions are imposed at the very last moment. Secular law, especially since society in Western democratic states became much stricter than it used to be in the 70s or early 80s of the last century, reacts more vigorously to illegal behaviour

than in the past, a reaction which includes the introduction of penal procedures in an early stage already.

To sum up, the failure of canon law with regard to child abuse by priests
can be explained by an interaction of two elements, namely the implicit
survival of the *societas perfecta* concept combined with a canonical legal
culture technically and ideologically hampered in running a proper penal
system.

II. Pressure exercised by state law

The weakness of the so called 'autonomous' canon law goes together with an
increasingly dominant position of the secular legal system.

In two different ways, the increasing importance of state law affects the
canonical system in general and its norms with regard to sexual abuse in particular. On the one hand, state law has a much larger scope than it used to
have in the past; on the other hand judges (and public opinion) are less
reluctant to apply existing norms in matters regarding churches and
religious groups.

1. The extended field of application of newly issued state law

One hundred years ago, secular legislation was considerably less ambitious
than it is today. Many fields in society were unregulated, left to the free
choice of its citizens. Some examples: labour law almost did not exist,
environmental law for a long time was a new issue, and competition law and
protection of consumers were only poorly developed. Fewer statutes and
more freedom: so far a summary of the legal situation in Western democra-
cies approximately one century ago.

Since legislation became more ambitious, logically, the scope of the
autonomy that churches enjoy decreased. For instance, labour law increasingly affects the position of those working for the church. In many countries,
only priests with a clear pastoral job are with certainty not bound by the
many compulsory labour law norms. The result of this evolution is obvious.
Canon law loses its monopoly position in determining the legal status of
people employed by the church.[10]

2. The extended field of application of existing state law

Secular case law increasingly requires the horizontal functioning of fundamental rights and the necessity of minimal legal standards in all groups that
are part of society, including religious groups.

With regard to child abuse by priests, jurisprudence concerning both liability and professional confidentiality affects churches and religious groups more than before. This evolution stimulates churches to adapt their legal norms in the direction of overall state law standards.

Liability is the first important problem forcing the church to adapt the norms shared by nearly all players in modern democratic society. Especially in the United States, where the financial consequences of liability are enormous, the church feels obliged to cope with the norms and policies set forward by secular society. Usually, attempts to limit liability have not been successful. Nonetheless, various attempts were made. A good example can be found in the Missouri Digital News of 27 January 1997. 'James Tierney, attorney for the Catholic Diocese of Kansas City-St Joseph, argued that the diocese cannot be held liable for sexual abuse by its priests because the hiring, firing, supervision and retention of the clergy is an ecclesiastical matter. "The relationships between churches and its clergy are different from the employer-employee relationships," said Tierney . . . The first Amendment gives churches absolute immunity from state incursion . . . Lack of such protection, he argued, would violate freedom of religious expression.'[11]

Ultimately, liability cases and burdensome settlements of claims led the United States Conference of Catholic Bishops (USCCB) to issue the *Essential Norms for Diocesan/Episcopal Policies Dealing with Allegations of Sexual Abuse of Minors by Priests or Deacons.*[12] These norms were approved by the Roman Congregation for Bishops on 8 December 2002. This approval is a sign of compatibility with the universal law of the Roman Catholic Church. Yet, already on 14 June of the same year, in Dallas, the USCCB issued other norms and a *Charter for the Protection of Children and Young People*[13] which did not obtain Roman approval. One of the underlying reasons is that the Dallas-norms included all necessary tools to counter successfully liability claims brought before state courts, but did not take into account sufficiently canon law and the requirements set forward by the CIC 1983.[14] In other words, church strategy went from one extreme to another. In a first stage, liability was challenged by the church on the level of principles, as it was perceived as being opposed to religious freedom. Later, it became clear that liability could only be avoided by establishing good internal norms and by applying them strictly. Consequently, state principles on liability became the cornerstone of any reform within the church, and at the same time internal canon law suddenly became of secondary importance.

Liability problems, of course, are not limited to the United States alone. We identify them also in other countries, such as Belgium, the Netherlands,

England, Ireland as well as many other countries belonging to the Western tradition.

Another sensitive topic is the protection of professional confidentiality, which differs from the seal of confession.

Here, an interesting case was dealt with by the tribunal of Caen (France). On 4 September 2001, Monsignor Pierre Pican, Bishop of Bayeux, was convicted to an imprisonment of three months (with delay) because he did not report one of his priests, Fr Bissey, to the state authorities. Monsignor Pican knew about child abuse committed by the latter. He sent him to a retirement home for some months, after which Bissey obtained an appointment in another parish. There, among other tasks, he was responsible for the Catholic youth (*Action de la jeunesse catholique*). Unfortunately, new acts of child abuse followed shortly afterwards.[15]

The court in Caen clearly made a choice in favour of the protection of the victims. Monsignor Pican, who knew about the facts even while ignoring the details, should have revealed these facts to state authorities. Professional confidentiality cannot be invoked as an excuse for not denouncing a priest committing child abuse.

On 7 September 2001, Monsignor Pican declared that he did not intend to appeal against the decision taken by the tribunal. He preferred to restore peace, both in his diocese and among the victims of Fr Bissey. Yet, in the same statement Monsignor Pican deplored the limitation of professional confidentiality resulting from the court decision.[16]

Clearly, the church will have to adapt its internal policy, including possibly its written norms, in order to avoid penal sanctions imposed by state courts.

The liability problem as well as the professional secrecy issue show how important internal dealing (by the church) with sexual abuse of minors is for the state. It equally makes clear that crucial changes in church order are often due to external pressure by state courts. This pressure entails more direct practical consequences than fascinating theological theories do.

III. Comments for the future

The slow and inadequate church policy with regard to child abuse led to a rather radical reaction by both secular courts and public opinion.

Nevertheless, this reaction, however justified, entails some risks. The reaction is fully adequate in sofar as it questions the position of the church as a *societas perfecta*, which considers itself as (almost) exempt from state law statutes. Such an approach is no longer acceptable. The state cannot allow the church to transgress morality and public order, and the church should adapt its internal statutes to its own teaching as developed by the Second Vatican Council.

But then again, the reaction can go too far. Enforcing mandatory secular statutes within the church should never lead to the abolition of church autonomy, nor should it endanger the free internal organization of churches and religious groups. When in recent years local churches tried, through issuing particular norms, to implement modern legal standards in church procedures concerning child abuse by priests, some commentators challenged the mere right of the church to establish such procedures. Why not leave child abuse by priests in its entirety to secular courts? This question was asked quite often by both the press and public opinion. Although the reaction is understandable, given the mistakes made in the past by church authorities, the suggested idea is not a good one. The church should not, and cannot, leave child abuse trials to secular tribunals alone. Moreover, some measures are irrelevant in the eyes of secular law, while canonically speaking they remain of utmost importance. In canon law, questions emerge such as: Will the priest be suspended? Can he be laicised? If so, which measures shall be taken in order to take care of him materially? Will he qualify for any other function or church office in the future? These questions cannot and should not be answered by state tribunals. In other words, there is a middle road between the church as an isolated *societas perfecta* and the church without any autonomy, deprived of any internal legal system. The latter has the right to survive; it should even be stimulated and developed more thoroughly, yet without hindering or influencing secular procedures of criminal charges where they arise.

In Belgium and in the Netherlands, the particular norms established a good compromise: as long as a secular trial is taking place the internal church procedure is suspended. This means that any danger of a 'parallel justice' is automatically eliminated. Yet, once the state court has taken a decision, the church can continue its internal procedure. It can, for instance, add a canonical penalty to a secular one which already has been imposed by the state court. And even if the priest has been acquitted by this court, he may remain guilty in the eyes of the church, as the canonical list of offenses is different from the secular one. Sexual intercourse by a priest with a consenting unmarried woman is not an offence in the state, yet it is in the church, where the priest is bound by the vow of celibacy.

I would like to express a final hope. An equilibrium between the church as a perfect society and the absence of any church autonomy will hopefully be found. Yet the church should be sincere in spelling out its future policy with regard to child abuse committed by priests. It should openly recognize the important influence exercised by state courts. The case law they produced led to the virtual end of the church as a *societas perfecta* approximately four decades after the ideological turnabout achieved by Vatican II. In any case, this secular influence is not something to be ashamed of: secular legal culture developed partly as a mix of canon law influences and moral requirements coming from Christianity. Moreover, as the church often offered good things to the state, why then should the opposite be peculiar or even impossible?

Unfortunately, some church leaders and their collaborators describe the current and future church policy as a logical result of true concern for victims of sexual abuse and as an inevitable consequence of theological ideas. They also focus on the importance of a thoroughly elaborated pastoral letter.[17] In other words, the usual techniques are highlighted once again, whereas the crucial role which has been played by state law is dramatically overlooked. This is not a good idea. People, including the Christian faithful, know very well why it was that the church finally changed its policy. Certainly, concern for the victims and theological ideas may have played a role for developing new strategies and policies. Yet, they were not the cornerstone of the paradigm shift. The real reason why new procedures were introduced was powerful state law and the fear experienced by church leaders of suffering severe sanctions. Ignoring this historical fact, could, *vis-à-vis* the church, lead to yet another presumption of hypocrisy. And that, certainly, is not a good outcome.

Notes

1. P. Granfield, 'The Rise and Fall of *Societas Perfecta*', *Concilium*, 1982, no. 7, pp. 3–9.
2. *Synopsis iuris ecclesiastici publici et privati quod per terras haereditarias augustissimae Mariae Thereresiae obtinet*, Vienna 1776, nr. 31.
3. C. Tarquini, *Iuris ecclesiastici publici institutiones*, Rome, Typis civilitatis catholicae, 1868, VIII + 149 pp.
4. F. Cavagnis, *Notions de droit public naturel et ecclésiastique*, Paris/Brussels: Desclée 1887, 202 e.s.
5. J. D. Mansi, *Sacrorum consiliorum nova et amplissima collectio*, LIII, Graz, Akademische Druck- und Verlaganstald 1961, p. 315.
6. Cf. R. Torfs, 'The Roman Catholic Church and Secular Legal Culture in the Twentieth Century', *Studia Historiae Ecclesiasticae*, 1999, vol. XXV, no. 1, p. 6.
7. P. Granfield, 'The Rise and Fall' (n. 1), p. 7.
8. L. Örsy, 'General Norms' in J. A. Coriden, T. I. Green and D. E. Heintschel (eds), *The Code of Canon Law. A Text and Commentary*, New York/Mahwah: Paulist Press 1985, p. 38.

9. Up until recently, dismissal from the clerical state has remained exceptional. It has to be formulated explicitly as a possible penalty by the universal legislator which happens in the canons 1364 §2; 1367; 1370 §1; 1387; 1394 §1; 1395.

10. R. Torfs, 'Les animateurs pastoraux en Europe' in A. Borras (ed), *Des laïcs en responsabilité pastorale?*, Paris: Cerf 1998, pp. 157–79.

11. See http://www.mdn.org/1997/STORIES/PRIESTS.HTM

12. See http://www.usccb.org/bishops/norms.htm

13. For more information see http://www.usccb.org/bishops/wiltonnews.htm

14. Cf. on this topic R. Torfs, 'Die Entlassung aus dem Klerikerstand im Strafrecht' in A. Weiss and S. Ihli (eds), *flexibilitas iuris canonici. Festschrift für Richard Puza zum 60. Geburtstag*, Frankfurt am Main: Peter Long 2003, pp. 183–485.

15. See e.g. http://www.humanité.fr/journal/2001–06–14/2001–06–14–245741

16. http://www.cef.fr/catho/actus/communiques/2001/commu20010907pican.plp4

17. Comp. L. De fleurquin, 'Pädophilie und "episkopein". Massnahmen der Bishofskonferenzen von England und Wales sowie von Irland und Schottland' in A. Weiss and S. Ihli (eds) (n. 17), p. 474.

Body of Power and Body Power:
The Situation of the Church and God's Defeat

RAINER BUCHER

The *Boston Herald* reports that the archdiocese of Boston is selling the archbishop's residence and the surrounding land, using the proceeds to compensate victims of sexual abuse by church workers. According to real estate experts, the building, dating from the 1920s, and the land are worth around $20 million. All in all the archdiocese faces claims of around $85 million. A large part of the sum is to be paid from insurance payments. By selling the building the archdiocese wants to show that the payments for victims of abuse 'are not coming from gifts or pastors' contributions', according to a spokesman.[1]

I. In ruins: the church as a powerful body[2]

Both Marxism and, in a somewhat more nobly restrained way, liberalism, expected the ruin of the churches in developed capitalist societies. Both seem to have got things somewhat wrong.

Nevertheless, the Catholic churches of the West are experiencing their situation as one of extreme crisis. This is not surprising, and it is right that they should do so. For example, the number of those involved in the Catholic Church, measured by the classical indicator of Sunday church attendance, has declined drastically since the 1950s in the countries of Western Europe. But above all the epoch-making change in the form of the socialization of the religious in developed society causes concern for the church. The 'use-pattern' of the church by its own members has changed fundamentally.

At the present time the 'Constantinian' constitution of the churches which had kept them stable and at the same time flexible since late antiquity, enabling them to survive every kind of historical shift, is collapsing. In the developed societies of the West the churches are changing from being more or less indispensable communities of fate into which one was born, socialized or even forced, to being suppliers to the market of providing meaning, helping to cope with life and find orientation in the world: they may still be strong and influential, but for some time they have also been dependent on success and on the market.

The project of civil society had already driven the church from its Olympian position in dominating society into the arena of the many social groups. The Catholic Church reacted to this in an essentially 'modern' way, if modern means adopting a strategy of projected self-formation. The Reformation had already encouraged this process, when for the first time the Catholic Church became its own concern at the moment of the greatest threat to it as an institution. With the collapse of the half-completed Catholic social and moral milieu from the middle of the twentieth century on, for the Catholic Church there then began what its leaders today see as a crisis for the church of the West: the loss of the monopoly among church members by the church authorities which provide religious orientation.

Neither internal personal sanctions, set up for example by means of a 'pastoral' approach based on fear, nor the threat of social ostracism compel people today to become involved with the church. Catholics who are quite accustomed to religious rule now feel that they can adopt a free attitude towards religion and its institutions. This 'invasion of modernity' hit the Catholic Church quite hard. It was somewhat surprised in the twentieth century to find that the institutional fortress which it had carefully erected and theologically secured in the middle of the nineteenth century had been razed to the ground. Above all the fact that their own members have permanent reservations about assenting to their teachings is causing the churches, and especially the Catholic Church, great difficulties.

Today the churches must learn painfully to live in the ruins of their former triumphal, but now shattered, systems of power. Now ruins lack two things above all: the connection which once existed between their parts when these were still parts of a whole, and a roof. Granted, the lost connection is still there as it was before – ruins are always ruins of something – but this something is present only as the image of a shattered past; therefore to those who live in them they permanently convey a certain gap in experience; they are perceived too much as the broken parts of what once was a whole.

Ruins also lack a roof. They no longer constitute a space of their own but are elements 'in the open air'. The outside world, which was once shut off, or to which access was controlled, is now constantly visible and forces itself in; it opens up broad prospects which those who always felt shut in welcome, but it also gives a sense of being unprotected, which is feared by those who seek protection and security in the sphere of religious institutions.

What is the future in such a situation? The churches of the West were inherited by prosperous modern states as providing a pastoral regulation of life, but institutionally somewhat over-proportioned and under-financed, given the diminishing number of their members and those participating in their activities. They stand in a religious landscape the features of which are not known precisely; it depends on whether one accepts the evidence of secularization or sees signs of a religious individualization and deinstitution-alization. At all events the churches are compelled to engage in nothing less than a quite far-reaching reinvention of themselves. The precarious partici-pation of their own members, who increasingly make their own biographies and the late-modern problems of coherence the primary points of reference for religious plausibilities and practices, is compelling the churches to undertake a comprehensive reshaping of their own constitutional principles. Here, looked at over long periods, they have experience of their own, but less time than before is available to them for their transformation.

II. Pastoral power

1. It is a form of power the goal of which is to secure the salvation of the individual soul in another world.
2. Pastoral power is not merely a form of power which commands; it must also be ready to sacrifice itself for the life and salvation of the flock. Here it differs from royal power, which requires the sacrifice from its subjects when the throne is to be saved.
3. It is a form of power which is concerned not only for the community as a whole but for each individual throughout his or her life.
4. One cannot exercise this form of power without knowing what is going on in people's heads, without searching their souls, without making them reveal their innermost secrets. It implies a knowledge of the conscience and a capacity to direct it.[3]

Thus in the West at the present time what Michel Foucault has usefully and in an analytically precise way called 'pastoral power' is finally leaving the churches. Within Christianity pastoral power was concentrated in the person of the 'shepherd', the one in office. As 'the only religion which has organized itself as a church . . . Christianity in principle argues that some individuals by virtue of their religious character are able to serve others, not as princes, judges, prophets, soothsayers, benefactors or educators, but as *pastors*. At any rate this word represents a quite distinct form of power.'[4]

In contrast with political power, pastoral power is orientated on the salvation of the individual's soul; unlike the power of the ruler it was unselfish, and in contrast to legal power it was not concerned with the valid-ity of universal rules, but with individuals. The pastoral power of the church extended over the whole of life, from cradle to grave. 'Whatever the shepherd does is directed towards the wellbeing of his flock. He is constantly concerned for it. While it sleeps, he keeps watch. This theme of keeping watch is important, as it brings out two aspects of the shepherd's dedication. First he acts, works, toils for those who are sleeping. Secondly he watches over them. He pays attention to all of them and loses sight of none of them.'[5]

Foucault points out that Christianity is thus based on a technique of power which was fundamentally different from the ancient techniques of power which preceded it and which is still used in the modern state. The modern state has adopted the originally Christian form of pastoral power, ultimately so successfully that it has taken over from the churches as the bearer of pastoral power. According to Foucault, in the eighteenth century pastoral power went over to the rising modern state – in its own double function of 'individualizing' and 'totalizing'. Never in the history of human societies has there been such a successful combination of techniques of individualization and procedures of totalization within one and the same political structure. However, the result is that the modern Western state has integrated the old Christian technique of power, pastoral power, into a new political form.

Here the primary approach of the church's pastoral power has led in a specific direction in modern times. It has led from the cosmos to community and finally to the body. That Christianity was self-evidently coded in the cosmos was first put in question by men like Galileo, Copernicus and Kepler; and the church's grasp on the community (outside the church) was lost with the project of civil society in the nineteenth century, after the absolutism of the eighteenth century had already largely freed itself from the horizons defined by the church. Last of all, the churches attempted still to influence the body and its practices and techniques, for example through their moral preaching.[6]

However, sexual abuse by priests perverts pastoral power at a time when it is evaporating. For these shepherds do not sacrifice themselves for their flock; parts of their flock sacrifice themselves for the shepherds.

III. Priests according to their power

Priests possess an office than which no higher can be conceived, so that they are rightly called not only angels but even gods, because they represent the power and loftiness of the immortal God among us . . .

So it is not to be doubted that their office [that of bishops and priests] is of such a kind that no higher than it can be conceived. Therefore it is not illegitimate for the bishops and priests to be called not only angels but also

Gods; because they bear in themselves the power and the glory of the immortal God.

(Roman Catechism)[7]

As is well known, priests are highly privileged in the Catholic Church, both theologically and legally. However, after the collapse of the church's cathedrals of power, their concrete professional role is being recognized less and less.

In the developed societies of the West the life of a priest is no longer lived in an unquestioned inner sphere, a realm of plausibility which is taken for granted. The church is no longer the sole authority for interpreting the world, and in a thoroughly modernized society it can no longer create an enclosed world to live in which has a traditional stamp. Its central personal structural element was the priestly hierarchy. But the strategy of securing the stability of the church by constructing a closed milieu within modern society centred on the priesthood has suddenly itself come to threaten the church's existence and not least the central personal element of this strategy, the priests.

The priest was strictly required to observe a specific ethic in accordance with his status, which demanded for example renunciation of marriage and family and also personal piety, humility, obedience and discreet leadership qualities. He used to get something in return: status and power, respect and a home, and even a sense of chosenness. In a word, he got recognition.

But when the walls of the milieu in which all this was true break down, the priest has to assert himself in the free arena of competing claims to validity and model biographies. And neither the theory nor the practice of the priesthood was orientated on this. Until well into the twentieth century the organizational idea for the church's hierarchy was not self-assertion in a free social arena, but internal stabilization by keeping clear of liberal society. The priests as the central and privileged representatives of this social form of the church are most affected by its end.

Today's priests must get by in a post-modern society[8] on the basis of a pre-modern theory of their priesthood but are measured – not least by their superiors – by the criteria for success in a modern competitive society. They also find themselves exposed to expectations from members of the church that they will pay sensitive attention to each individual's biography. The parish priest is now more or less torn apart between his role as a sacrally legitimated mediator of salvation; the demands of being a regional 'local representative' of a worldwide religious institution, the 'Catholic Church'; and the pressure of the expectations of individual faithful that they will receive therapeutic help and support in life.

Even today the priest is still ultimately burdened legally with responsibility for the community. But he no longer has any possibilities of influence corresponding to his status in church law and theology, as he did in the nineteenth century. For in the eyes of most of the faithful the priest no longer derives his authority primarily from his sacramental and hierarchical status but from his pastoral and professional competence.[9] Thus above all the parish priest has become the victim of the epoch-making changes in the social form of the Catholic Church which can be observed today. Instead of being the sacrally legitimated guarantor of church authority he is torn between different claims, even within the social sphere of the church.

IV. Body power: God's defeat

> Sexual violence is a phenomenon less of sex than of power. Interrogations of perpetrators and victims show that the perpetrators are primarily interested in exercising power in order to feel superior, to humiliate, to punish, to vent anger or to prove their own masculinity. Sexuality is merely a means – a very effective means – of doing this.[10]

Sexual abuse in the framework of pastoral activity is an attack, a breach of trust, and – because of the inequality of power expressed in it (adult–child; pastor–person being cared for) – a phenomenon of the use of power at a sensitive point. And it is a defeat for God in the action of the people of God and its priests.

For Christian pastoral care is not just any action, but action as disciples of Jesus and his preaching of God. One of the central statements of this message stands in the Beatitudes of the Sermon on the Mount: 'Blessed are the poor, for theirs is the kingdom of God. Blessed are the hungry, for they shall be filled. Blessed are those who weep, for they shall laugh' (Luke 6.20–21).

Here the poor, the hungry and those who weep are praised without any religious qualification in the narrower sense. The eschatological salvation announced is theirs. The promised salvation of the kingdom of God may indeed in its fullness be a future eschatological entity; however, it is not only decided here and now with God, but also already has an influence on the present, on the little ones, the powerless, those who weep. For and in Jesus, God and God's political secular dimension, his kingdom, become concrete. They become concrete in the world of proclaiming this God and in the concrete actions of Jesus' care for those who need support, healing and help. All pastoral work is a matter of following these actions of Jesus.

Therefore Christian pastoral care is first and foremost diaconia; it is offering help as disciples of Jesus in accordance with his message of the kingdom of God.[11] An essential element in Christian pastoral care is concern for those in need. Unless this is element is part of it, pastoral care is not grounded in the action of its founder. Pastoral care, the care of souls, is a creative confrontation between the present and the gospel.[12] In its pastoral care the church has to represent Jesus and the loving-kindness of his God[13] in word and deed.

Faith plays a role in the living of any human life, and consciousness is not the primary place where this faith is to be found. 'What you set your heart on and bring about . . . is really your God,' wrote Luther.[14] However, faith can be recognized most clearly in the actions and accomplishments of one's own life. Our faith is what we live by, what we ultimately depend on, what we really trust in our decisions and everyday actions.

Jesus' concept of God is a central principle in Christian pastoral care. Jesus criticizes all gods who oppress human life. As is well known, there are many of them in any life. Pastoral competence means asking about the God and the gods of one's own life or that of others and being able to look at one's own gods in the light of the God of Jesus. Do the gods of one's own life enslave one or liberate one for a brave life which is rich in experiences, for a life (one's own and that of others) that is true and intense in relationships, bold and adventurous, but above all one which is honest and builds up the lives of others?

Developed modernity has stripped the church of almost all social and religious power. Sexual abuse in pastoral work diminishes that in another way, with other means, and in the most intimate place conceivable – for whatever individual reasons.[15] Sexual abuse is a setback for what the church has finally achieved consistently after a thousand years of a 'Constantinian formation' and thus the power of social sanctions, namely pastoral care as the free promise, the diaconal help of the God of Jesus in word of action, unselfish and without ulterior motives, simply because that is what God's universal will wants it to be.

Pastoral care is liberation from the false gods of life, but sexual abuse in pastoral care establishes these very false gods: first and brutally the god of power. Sexual abuse in pastoral care speaks actively of the god of a forced intimacy which has crept in, a god who confuses proximity induced by power with love, a god who is perverse in the strict sense. This god of violence and power (hidden or manifest) has always existed in the church, even though God has really driven him out once and for all.

Pastoral care is liberation from the false gods of life, from the petty and poor gods of a life which is all too cosy and self-satisfied. For God calls on us to lead this one and unique life with complete seriousness and intensity, as a venture for God and our fellow human beings and in the certainty of faith that we shall never ever be submerged either in the cold of the silent cosmos or in the cold of human hate. Where pastors abuse children they proclaim a god of (sexual) faint-heartedness who upsets the balance of power in intimate human relationships, they proclaim a God who sends children into the cold of simulated intimacy and experiences which are hard to cope with, if they can be coped with at all.

Pastoral care is liberation from the blinding and seductive god of an assertive over-estimation of oneself, for we are not the gods of our own life, nor do we even make that life; rather, everything that is really important for us, from our sheer existence to the love of another, is purely and ultimately an unmerited gift. Where pastors abuse children, they proclaim a God who allows the authorities to do anything, even the impermissible; who makes love and affection dependent on compliance and the offering of a sacrifice. Where pastors abuse children they represent the seductive God of heedless self-glorification.

Pastoral care is liberation from the gods of a lack of self-confidence and self-control that make people ill; from unending mourning, oppressive family and kinship relationships, and fettering dependencies. For we are the beloved children of God, who does not want us to be unhappy but to lead our lives to the full, also and precisely in our guiltiness, which is completely unavoidable. Where pastors abuse children they proclaim a god of oppressive dependencies in the most intimate sphere, a god who then all too often makes people sick, destroys self-confidence and autonomy, and does not take away guilt but imposes guilt-feelings.

Pastoral care is liberation from the diverse gods of human and religious repression. For the God of Jesus is a God of freedom and the fight for the outcast, a God who offers those who really fall outside all frameworks of recognition his complete and utter solidarity: the 'morally dubious', the incurable ill, the 'unclean',[16] children, those unable to work. Where pastors abuse children, they proclaim a god who blatantly is none of these things: who is a god not of freedom but of power, a god who does not fight for the outcast but produces outcasts, a god not of children, but of adults.

According to Jesus we know one thing above all about God: Jesus radically identifies love of our God with love of our fellow human beings: 'If anyone says "I love God" but hates his brother, he is a liar' (I John 4.19). All gods which enslave men and women, rob them of their freedom and make them ill, are idols; they may be powerful and effective, but Christian pastoral care joins battle with them. Where pastors abuse children, this battle is already almost lost.

Idols are powers over our lives which function in the interest either of state or religious rule or of a 'good life' for the individual, his or her self-satisfied contentment, his or her liberated existence. By contrast Christian pastors have to present a God who is in principle not at our disposal, who remains a mystery: the mystery of our life which infinitely transcends us. Pastoral care is then the presentation of this God in the concrete realities of individual biographies. But sexual abuse by pastors is an active denial of God in the concrete realities of individual biographies – in the very context where it is claimed that witness is being borne to God.

The God of Jesus is the great hope in the life of every individual, for God teaches us to see the world with other eyes. This God criticizes the idols and shows solidarity with sufferers. This God is under no one's control. This God is not a God of power but of solidarity with the helpless.[17] Sexual abuse in the context of pastoral care is the opposite: it is part of God's defeat in his church.

Translated by John Bowden

Notes

1. *Süddeutsche Zeitung*, 5 December 2003, p. 8.
2. For what follows see in more detail R. Bucher, 'Entmonopolisierung und Machtverlust. Wie kam die Kirche in die Krise?' in id. (ed), *Die Provokation der Krise. Zwölf Fragen und Antworten zur Lage der Kirche*, Würzburg 2004, pp. 11–29.
3. M. Foucault, 'Warum ich Macht untersuche? Die Frage des Subjekts' in H. Dreyfus and P. Rabinov, *Jenseits von Strukturalismus und Hermeneutik*, Frankfurt am Main 1987, pp. 243–50: 248.
4. Ibid.
5. M. Foucault, 'Omnes et singulatim. Zu einer Kritik der politischen Vernunft' in J. Vogl (ed), *Gemeinschaften. Positionen zu einer Philosophie des Politischen*, Frankfurt am Main 1994, pp. 65–93: 69f.
6. How little the church's pastoral power is still effective, how much the balance of power has changed, is evident not least from the fact that, say, in Germany Catholic moral preaching finds little assent even with most church members. Cf. Medien-DienstleistungsGmbH, *Trendmonitor Religiöse Kommunikation*, München-Allensbach 2003, pp. 49–55.
7. Roman Catechism, German edition, Part 2, Vienna 1763, p. 448.
8. Here this simply means a society in which the present is not, as in pre-modern times, given the task of following a (normative and idealized past), and does not, as in the modern period which has recently come to an end, understand itself as the prehistory to a (normative and idealized) future, but is a place where the

main conern is to regulate its own conflicts, which tend to be incapable of resolution, with as little violence as possible, or at least to put up with them.

9. Cf. e.g. the results of the empirical study by: J. B. A. M. Schilderman, J. A. van der Ven and A. J. A. Felling, 'Professionalising the Shepherds', *JET* 12, 1999, pp. 59–90.

10. U. Brockhaus and M. Kolshorn, 'Die Ursachen sexueller Gewalt' in G. Amann and R. Wipplinger (eds), *Sexueller Missbrauch. Überblick zu Forschung, Beratung und Therapie*, Tübingen ²1998, pp. 89–105: 91.

11. See O. Fuchs, *Der Dienst am Nächsten als Ernstfall von Kirche und Pastoral*, Düsseldorf 1990.

12. See R. Bucher, 'Die pastorale Konstitution der Kirche. Was soll Kirche eigentlich?' in id. (ed), *Die Provokation der Krise* (n.2), pp. 30–44.

13. See K. Bopp, *Barmherzigkeit im pastoralen Handeln der Kirche*, Munich 1998.

14. *Martin Luthers Grosser Katechismus* (1529) ed G. Herrmann, Gütersloh 1961, p. 15.

15. Of course this does not exclude, but rather includes, the fact that even, indeed precisely, in times when the church still had power and in places where it was still engaged widely in education, for example in homes for children, given the conditions there were such attacks.

16. For all the great involvement of the church in ministry which is shown in its history, this history is also a history of guilt with which the church must come to terms, particularly in connection with religious and moral 'deviants'. Here too, no liberation for new action is possible without recognition of one's own guilt.

17. Cf. H.-J. Sander, *Nicht verleugnen. Die befremdende Ohnmacht Jesu*, Würzburg 2001; id., *Macht in der Ohnmacht. Eine Theologie der Menschenrechte*, Freiburg im Breisgau etc. 1999.

Postscript

REGINA AMMICHT QUINN, HILLE HAKER
AND MAUREEN JUNKER-KENNY

'I supposed Him to exist only within the walls of a church – in fact, of our church – and I also supposed that God and safety were synonymous. The word "safety" brings us to the real meaning of the word "religious" as we use it' (James Baldwin).[1]

> *We apologize to the victims. We are grateful to them for their courage in breaking silence. We are ashamed of the transgressions of our church and demand that the victims and the priests who have become perpetrators experience justice and not just 'compensation' and 'rejection'.*

The crisis in which the Catholic Church finds itself as a result of offences against children and young people is *our* crisis. We are members of a church which – once again – has kept silent; it has covered up men who have damaged the psychological health of children irreparably; for years it has kept quiet about offences which elsewhere immediately involve the courts. Much has been written and discovered in recent years; as members of the church and as part of the general public there is much that we still do not know.

What we know is this. We are dealing with a twofold and ambiguous catastrophe. Children and young people are being made the victims, in the most sensitive and most intimate parts of their identity conceivable, of those who are meant to guide and protect them; these victims have been betrayed by those who as a community want to establish a sign of holiness in the world.

Trust is a necessary element of any living church. Here this trust has been abused at two levels of the catastrophe. We do not yet know whether it has finally been destroyed. The betrayal of the victims is at the same time also the betrayal of trust in the representatives of the church, who by virtue of their office have the special responsibility of giving *ethical* shape to their authority. The betrayal of trust is a betrayal of the insight that priests and bishops must make ethical responsibility towards those with whom they communicate as priests and bishops the criterion of their action; otherwise their authority becomes an authoritarian exercise of power which is unworthy of a church.

This betrayal, which is expressed in each individual case involving violence and which has continued in the way in which the church and its bishops has dealt with the perpetrators, does not only shake us personally: it shakes the very foundations of the church as the place of discipleship of Christ.

Except that the church is not shaken. Financial payments, the resignations of bishops, the removal of priests from office – all these are very necessary steps, though often enough they have not been granted the victims as a matter of course, but have had to be and still have to be fought for through wearisome legal proceedings. Many of the faithful are shaken as individuals; but whether this shaking goes beyond feelings of personal shock to become a shaking of the structures seems doubtful. We cannot avoid the impression that here a problem is being 'dealt with': some procedures have been changed, but otherwise the fundamental questions are being avoided. These fundamental questions are questions about the structure of a church based on a hierarchy which cannot be questioned by 'outsiders' and which as a result gives rise to structurally 'appropriate' mentalities – on the part of those who hold office and those who are dependent on them.

Instead of these questions being raised and worked on, in recent years in particular the position of the priest in the liturgy and in leadership of the community has been further strengthened, so that a hierarchical structure has been defended against a communicative structure. Thus, necessary as individual steps towards uncovering acts of violence and dealing with them are, they cannot solve the problem which we have put at the centre. What is happening to a church which many people no longer trust? How is it to treat people who continue to trust it, the church, and its priests? Priests – not just priests, but *also* priests, and in some respects above all priests – often meet children, young people and adults in threshold situations which have a high degree of intimacy. In these situations – in giving support in difficult situations in life, in the care of the sick or at funerals, but also in the sacramental practice of holy communion, penance or weddings – trust is an essential element in making the practice of faith possible at all. If this trust is lacking, the practice of faith turns into a phantom, a semblance of itself.

For a long period in the history of the church, trust in the relationship between priests and believers was brought about by structure alone – not through the personality but through the office and a mutual understanding that this office, and not the person of the priest, was decisive for the interaction. However, in this form this structural understanding of the priest as mediator has long ceased to apply; it has been replaced by an individualized understanding in which the priest takes on authority by virtue of both his office and his person. Only as a result of this is he in a position to cope with the uncertainties which often go along with threshold situations. The ethical authority of the priest which, despite all the emphasis on the people of God and the Spirit at Vatican II, in the understanding of the Catholic Church still stands at the centre of the interactions of faith, is particularly striking in doubly asymmetrical relationships, i.e. relationships which are asymmetrical not only through the structure of interaction with the church hierarchy, but in addition also through the particular vulnerability of one side. This particular asymmetry is always present in the case of children and young people. It can also be found in other contexts like kindergartens or schools. But there staff and teachers are subject to special control. Interference or violence is immediately punished as soon as it is detected. In the case of the asymmetrical relationships in the church, many bishops, as responsible authorities, have long acted in accordance with the motto: 'What may not happen does not happen, and if it does happen, then we shall say nothing about it, otherwise it would happen.' In this strategy there are offenders, but they are hidden or made invisible by admonitions, moves, or, today, dismissals. The ones who have long been outside the view of bishops are the victims.

If priests have betrayed the trust of those who have been entrusted to them, then the bishops who share responsibility for the priests have betrayed believers in two ways: they have 'forgotten' them, and they have left them alone with the priests concerned. For the victims the first betrayal is decisive. For us, the members of the church, the second betrayal is incomprehensible and intolerable: it is not based on the action of 'individuals', priests of whom possibly too much is being asked, who sometimes are also sick, but on a contempt for the faithful which has become part of the structure. This is betrayal at the heart of what the church is about: betrayal of discipleship of Christ.

Bishops have seen themselves – sometimes exclusively – as being responsible for their priests, whom often enough they have protected. Evidently they have not perceived any responsibility beyond their own power structure, a responsibility for the weak and the damaged, since this would have meant taking the victims and protection of the faithful seriously long before the brave publication of the accusations.

But now it is only such a responsibility for the weak which distinguishes the ethical authority of the priest from a position of power which makes use of violence. Authority turns into power when the vulnerability of others is exploited in order to gain advantages for oneself, of whatever kind. Sexual violence by priests against those dependent on them is based on such an abuse of authority, which turns into power. Priests who exercise their power over and through sexuality – sexuality which in their identity as Catholic priests they (must) in practice renounce – not only commit a criminal action and fail to do justice to their chosen identity, but in addition also violate the institution of the priestly office as an ethical authority, and they destroy the message for which they stand as individuals and those ordained to an office in the church.

So what is required of the church?

It must ask itself how the ethical authority of priests can be restored. This question cannot be understood solely as a question of the individual identity of those who have decided for and continue to decide for the priesthood. It is also a question to the institution: the training, support and control of priests in the exercise of their office is one thing; the structural shaping of the interaction between priests and the faithful is another; the theological and ecclesiological question of the form of the church is a third.

We, the editors of this issue, are theologians. We are women. We are mothers. Often enough, from the perspective of traditional church structures, we stand on 'the other side', though we are not the ones who define where the boundaries are drawn. We are Christian women, Catholics, members of communities in which our children too ought to have and find a place. We cannot and will not tolerate structures which allow individual priests and bishops to violate or even destroy people's psychological health. We cannot and will not tolerate decisions and practices which are more orientated on the preservation of authoritarian relationships than on the possibility of experiences and practices of faith, which put people's vulnerability at the centre.

Nor can we and will we tolerate priests who have gone beyond the bounds of any decent dealings with children and young people not being brought to justice. This justice can be sought only in proceedings which are located outside the entanglements of a particular situation, as should happen in any case of sexual violence; in our case this means that the proceedings must take place outside the church.

Here priests cannot simply be expelled from the institution in which they have lived and worked, often for decades. The responsibility of the church does not end with handing over the evidence to the relevant courts. In many modern legal systems there is punishment – for the sake of the victim – and rehabilitation – for the sake of the perpetrator. In dealing with the priests involved the church must do justice to both aspects. With concern and indignation we note how, in reaction to the cases of sexual violence in the church, in the contexts of both church and society sexual violence is associated with homosexuality. The fact that often, but not exclusively, boys and young men become victims must not become a pretext for reviving deep-seated prejudices and criminalizing homosexuality – as though on the basis of their sexual orientation homosexuals were more inclined to do violence to minors than heterosexuals. We dissociate ourselves from this suggestion, which is absurd, though often expressed – and we expect our church to do the same, openly and clearly.

It is equally unhelpful to identify sexual violence sweepingly with illness or paedophilia. There may very well be a connection between psychological disturbances and sexual violence, but this cannot be generalized and used as an excuse. The one thing that is clear is that the perpetrators, too, need to work through their offences therapeutically.

The problem of sexual violence may be more striking in the Western churches than in the non-Western churches. But does this mean that 'only' in the Western local churches is there a structure of authority which prevents individual and structural violence to children and young people, and in the end also to adults in dependent relationships, being recognized and fought against? If the answer is in the affirmative, then local churches in the West have critical helpers in the churches of the South towards bringing about the structural changes that are needed. If the answer is in the negative, then here the whole church has the responsibility of fundamentally rethinking church structures and gaining a new vision of the church. The question of the ethical authority of priests cannot (only) be understood as a question of virtue or attitude; it must be grasped as a structural problem of the identity and role of priests, as a problem of social interaction in asymmetrical relationships, and as a problem of the function of the bishops in control and protection.

We are only at the beginning of this process, which compels us to tackle the problems where they in fact arise; it is the beginning of a process which compels us to rethink the relationship between priests and believers, to improve the structures of control, and to raise once again the question of the ethical authority of priests.

In a situation in which the loss of relevance of the Christian churches is staggering, the question of the survival of the Christian message as a message which shapes individuals and cultures arises. Sexual violence which is committed in the church and through church power structures takes the loving-kindness of this Christian message to absurd extremes. Only conversion in the biblical sense could ward off what Rainer Bucher has called 'God's defeat in his church'.

Translated by John Bowden

Note
1. James Baldwin, 'Down at the Cross. Letter from a Region of My Mind' in *The Fire Next Time*, New York 1962.

Contributors

REGINA AMMICHT-QUINN studied Catholic theology and German and then did her dissertation and habilitation in theological ethics. She lectures on theological ethics at the Interfaculty Centre for Ethics in the sciences in Tübingen. Her publications include *Von Lissabon bis Auschwitz. Zum Paradigmawechsel in der Theodizeefrage*, Freiburg 1991 and *Körper – Religion – Sexualität. Theologische Reflexionen zur Ethik der Geschlechter*, Mainz ²2000.

Address: Humboldtstrasse 1, D-60318 Frankfurt, Germany
E-mail: regina.ammicht-quinn@t-online.de

HILLE HAKER is Professor of Christian Ethics at Harvard Divinity School. She studied Catholic theology, German and philosophy in Tübingen, Nijmegen and Munich. From 1992 to 2002 she was an academic assistent and senior assistant to the professor of ethics and social ethics in the Catholic theological faculty of the University of Tübingen. Publications include *Literarische Lebensgeschichten als Medium ethischer Reflexion. Mit einer Interpretation der 'Jahrestage' von Uwe Johnson*, Tübingen 1999; and *Ethik der genetischen Frühdiagnostik. Sozialethische Reflexionen zur Verantwortung am Beginn des menschlichen Lebens*, Paderborn 2002.

Address: Harvard Divinity School, 45 Francis Avenue, Cambridge MA 02138, USA
E-mail: hhaker@hds.harvard.edu

MAUREEN JUNKER-KENNY is Associate Professor of Theology at Trinity College, Dublin, where she teaches practical theology and Christian ethics in the School of Hebrew, Biblical and Theological Studies. Her research interests are in theological theories of action, biomedical ethics, and conditions for faith in late modernity. She has written on Schleiermacher's christology and theory of religion (Berlin 1990); on the philosophical and theological critiques of Habermas's ethics of argumentation (Stuttgart

1998), on *Designing Life? Genetics, Procreation, and Ethics* (Aldershot 1999) and on Ricoeur's ethics of remembering and forgiving (Münster 2003).

Address: School of Hebrew, Biblical and Theological Studies, Trinity College, Dublin 2, Ireland
E-mail: maureen.junker-kenny@tcd.ie

MARIE L. COLLINS is a founder member of the depression support organization 'Aware', where she has been a voluntary helpline counsellor for ten years. She is a director of 'One in Four', a support group for those who have suffered sexual abuse, and a member of the Lynott Working Group, which is drafting child protection guidelines for the Catholic Church in Ireland. She has written articles in the *Irish Times* and the *Irish Examiner* and has given papers on child sexual abuse, child pornography and child exploitation at conferences held at universities, hospital trusts and Barnado's in both parts of Ireland, Great Britain and the United States. She has been married for twenty-eight years and has one son.

Address: 12 Carriglea Court, firhouse, Dublin 24, Ireland
E-mail: mariecollins@ntlworld.ie

NANCY NASON-CLARK is Professor of Sociology at the University of New Brunswick in Fredericton, Canada. She is the author of *The Battered Wife: How Christians Confront Family Violence* (1997), and co-author with Catherine Clark Kroeger of *No Place for Abuse: Biblical and Practical Resources to Counteract Domestic Violence* (2001) and *Refuge from Abuse: Hope and Healing for Abused Christian Women* (forthcoming); she is co-editor of *Understanding Abuse: Partnering for Change* (with M. L. Stirling, C. A. Cameron and B. Miedema, 2004) and *Feminist Narratives and the Sociology of Religion* (with M. J. Neitz, 2001). She is also editor of the journal *Sociology of Religion: A Quarterly Review.*

LANETTE RUFF is a PhD student in the Department of Sociology at the University of New Brunswick in Canada. Her dissertation focusses on parenting styles of religious men and women.

Address: Department of Sociology, University of New Brunswick, PO Box 4400, Fredericton, NB, Canada E3B 5A3
E-mail: nasoncla@unb.   caLanette_Ruff@rogers.com

PETER ADRIAENSSENS was born in 1954. He is a medical doctor and has been Professor of Child and Adolescent Psychiatry at the University Hospital of Gasthuisberg (Leuven) and Director of the Confidential Centre on Child Abuse and Neglect since 1993. He has published widely in Dutch, French, English and German on child psychiatry, education and child abuse. In 1996, at the time of the 'Dutroux' case, he was invited by the Belgian King Albert II to be a national expert analysing the defects in the Belgian approach to child sexual abuse, and published his conclusions with a commission of six experts.

Address: University Hospital Gasthuisberg, Dept of Child Psychiatry, Herestraat 49, 3000 Leuven
E-mail: Peter.Adriaenssens@uzleuven.be

TRACI C. WEST is Associate Professor of Ethics and African American Studies at Drew University. She is the author of *Wounds of the Spirit: Black Women, Violence, and Resistance Ethics* (New York 1999), as well as many articles on violence against women, sexuality, welfare policy, and racial justice. She is an ordained minister in the United Methodist church who has previously served in campus and parish ministry.

Address: Drew University Theological School, 36 Madison Avenue, Madison, NJ, 07940, USA
E-mail: twest@drew.edu

ANDREAS MICHEL studied Catholic theology and history in Freiburg, Jerusalem and Tübingen. He gained his doctorate in 1996 in Catholic theology and his habilitation in 2003 in Old Testament at the Catholic theological faculty of the University of Tübingen. He now lectures at the University of Mainz.

Address: FB 01: Katholische Theologie, Seminar für Altes Testament, Universität Mainz, D-55099 Mainz, Germany
E-mail: amichel@mail.uni-mainz.de

HUBERTUS LUTTERBACH was born in 1961. He gained his doctorate in 1991, and his habilitation in church history in 1997. He spent several years in the USA and since 2000 has been Professor of the History of Christianity and Culture in the department of Catholic theology in the University of Essen. Recent publications on the topic are *Sexualität im Mittelalter. Eine Kulturstudie anhand von Bussbüchern des 6. bis 12. Jahrhunderts*, Archiv für

Kulturgeschichte. Beihefte 43, Cologne and Weimar 1999; *Religion und Terror. Stimmen zum 11. September 2001 aus Christentum, Islam und Judentum* (ed with Jürgen Manemann), Münster 2002; *Gotteskindschaft. Kultur- und Sozialgeschichte eines christlichen Ideals*, Freiburg, Basle and Vienna 2003.

Address: Fachbereich Katholische Theologie, Universität Essen, Universitätsstrasse 12, 45141 Essen, Germany
E-mail: hu.lu@gmx.de

EAMONN CONWAY is a priest of the diocese of Tuam, Senior Lecturer and Head of Theology and Religious Studies at Mary Immaculate College, University of Limerick, where he also co-directs the Centre for Culture, Technology and Values. He is author of *The Anonymous Christian – A Relativized Christianity? An evaluation of Hans Urs von Balthasar's Criticisms of Karl Rahner's Theory of the Anonymous Christian* (Peter Lang 1993), and has edited a number of books including *Twin Pulpits: Essays in Media and Church* (Veritas 1997), *The Splintered Heart* (Veritas 1998), *Child Sexual Abuse and the Catholic Church – A Pastoral Response* (Columba Press 1999), and *Technology and Transcendence* (Columba Press 2003).

Address: Theology and Religious Studies, Mary Immaculate College, University of Limerick, Ireland
E-mail: eamonn.conway@mic.ul.ie

JOHN P. BEAL is a presbyter of the Diocese of Erie, Pennsylvania, where he served as judicial vicar from 1984 to 1992. He earned a doctorate in Canon Law from the Catholic University of America, Washington, DC in 1985. Since 1992, he has been teaching canon law at the Catholic University, where he is now an associate professor. He is co-editor and major contributor to *A New Commentary on the Code of Canon Law* (Mahwah, NJ 2000), and has written 'The Exercise of Power of Governance by Lay People: The State of the Question', *The Jurist* 55 (1995), pp. 1–92, and 'It Shall Not Be So Among You! Crisis in the Church, Crisis in Church Law', in *Governance, Accountability and the Future of the Catholic Church*, New York 2004, pp. 88–102.

Address: School of Canon Law, The Catholic University Washington, DC 20064
E-mail: beal@cua.edu

HANS-JÜRGEN GUTH lectures in church law at the Catholic Theological Faculty of the University of Tübingen. His publications include *Ehescheidung oder Ehenichtigkeit? Das Eheprozessrecht der römisch-katholischen Kirche in den U.S.A. seit dem Zweiten Vatikanischen* Konzil, Freiburg, Switzerland 1993; *Kirchenasyl. Probleme – Konzepte – Erfahrungen* (with Monika Rappenecker), Mössingen-Talheim 1996; *IUS REMONSTRAN-DI. Das Remonstrationsrecht des Diözesanbischofs im kanonischen Recht*, Freiburg, Switzerland 1999.

Address: Katholisches Dekanat Balingen, Heilig Geist-Kirchplatz 2, D-72336 Balingen, Deutschland
E-mail: info@dekanat-balingen.de.

RIK TORFS was born in 1956. He received licentiates in Law and Notarial Science and a doctorate in Canon Law from the Catholic University of Leuven, where he has been professor since 1988 and Dean of the Faculty of Canon Law from 1994–2003. He has been Visiting Professor at the universities of Utrecht, Strasbourg, Stellenbosch, and Nijmegen, and is a member of the editorial boards of the *Revue de Droit Canonique (RDC), European Consortium for State-Church Research*, editor of the *European Journal for Church and State Research*, and a member of the Belgian government's 2004 Commission on Intercultural Dialogue. His publications on law and canon law, law, church and state relationships include *De vrouw en het kerkelijk ambt. Analyse in functie van de mensenrechten in Kerk en Staat*, Leuven 1985; *Het huwelijk als levensgemeenschap. Een kerkrechtelijke benadering*, Leuven 1990, *Congregationele gezondheidsinstellingen. Toekomstige structuren naar profaan en kerkelijk recht*, Leuven 1992; *A Healthy Rivalry: Human Rights in the Church*, Leuven and Grand Rapids, MI 1995; and *De kardinaal heft verdriet*, Leuven 2002.

E-mail: Rik.Torfs@law.kuleuven.ac.be

RAINER BUCHER was born in Nuremberg in 1956. He studied German and theology in Freiburg im Breisgau and Würzburg, and gained his doctorate in theology in 1986. After holding various posts in the University of Bamberg, he gained his habilitation there in 1996 in pastoral theology, and since 1990 he has been Professor of Pastoral Theology and Kerygmatics there, since 2000 head of the Institute for Pastoral Theology and Pastoral Psychology at the University of Graz. Publications include: *Nietzsches Mensch und Nietzsches Gott. Das Spätwerk als philosophisch-theologisches Programm*, Frankfurt am Main, Berne and New York ²1993; *Kirchenbildung in der*

Moderne. Eine Untersuchung der Konstitutionsprinzipien der deutschen katholischen Kirche im 20. Jahrhundert, Stuttgart 1998; *Theologie in den Kontrasten der Zukunft*, Graz 2001; *Die Provokation der Krise*, Würzburg 2004; and *Prophetie in einer etablierten Kirche* (with R. Korckauer), Münster 2004.

Address: Parkstrasse 1, A-8010 Graz, Austria
E-mail: R.Bucher@t-online.de

The editors would like to thank the following people for their help in preparing this issue:
Alberto Antoniazzi, Erik Borgman, Paulo Fernando Carneiro de Andrade, James A. Coriden, Virgil Elizondo, Rosino Gibellini, Thomas J. Green, M. Catherine Hilkert, Alberto Melloni, Teresa Okure, David N. Power, Paul Schotsmans, Brian Tierney, Rik Torfs

Concilium Subscription Information

February   2004/1: *Original Sin*

April   2004/2: *Rethinking Europe*

June   2004/3: *The Structural Betrayal of Trust*

October   2004/4: *African Christianities*

December   2004/5: *Feminist Movements in Different Religions*

New subscribers: to receive *Concilium 2004* (five issues) anywhere in the world, please copy this form, complete it in block capitals and send it with your payment to the address below.

Please enter my subscription for *Concilium 2004*

Individuals   Institutions
____ £32.50 UK/Rest of World   ____ £48.50 UK/Rest of World
____ $63.00 North America   ____ $93.50 North America
Please add £17.50/$33.50 for airmail delivery

Payment Details:
Payment must accompany all orders and can be made by cheque or credit card
I enclose a cheque for £/$ ____ Payable to SCM-Canterbury Press Ltd
Please charge my Visa/MasterCard (Delete as appropriate) for £/$ ____
Credit card number ....
Expiry date ....
Signature of cardholder ....
Name on card ....
Telephone .... E-mail ....

Send your order to *Concilium*, SCM-Canterbury Press Ltd
9–17 St Albans Place, London N1 ONX, UK
Tel +44 (0)20 7359 8033 Fax +44 (0)20 7359 0049
E-Mail: office@scm-canterburypress.co.uk

Customer service information:
All orders must be prepaid. Subscriptions are entered on an annual basis (i.e. January to December) No refunds on subscriptions will be made after the first issue of the Journal has been despatched. If you have any queries or require information about other payment methods, please contact our Customer services department.